THE SAVOY COOKBOOK

THE SAVOY COOKBOOK

Anton Edelmann

with Kate Whiteman

Photography by Jean Cazals

PAVILION

Contents

Foreword

After 35 years in the business, I can safely say that there is no such thing as a perfect hotel or kitchen. However, after 21 years here at The Savoy I can assert that this hotel often comes close to this elusive state. Of course, many elements contribute to perfection in a hotel or kitchen. At The Savoy, these include its style, its special atmosphere, its history and architecture, the quality of service and food, and the attitude and passion of the people who work here. But above all, it is our guests who make it so special. They see The Savoy as the quintessential English hotel.

Perfection can only be achieved by looking at every minute detail time and time again! In a kitchen or restaurant there are many mundane and repetitive jobs, such as filleting fish, peeling vegetables, folding napkins and polishing glasses. It is difficult to stay motivated when you perform the same relatively simple task every day, yet it is important to do it well and always seek ways to improve it.

This becomes easier and more pleasurable if you are dealing with only the best quality. Handling the freshest asparagus, the smallest, crispest beans, or filleting fish so fresh that it still has rigor mortis, feeling the firmness of new season's lamb or a plump organic chicken – then it is easy to see where the pleasure comes from.

I am often asked how to cut corners in cooking. My answer is always the same. Cooking is about taking the time to create something that will bring pleasure to others. It is not to follow a recipe as closely as possible – you must be passionate about what you are doing. Then a simple soup or a flavoursome stew may turn into a masterpiece.

It is this, I believe, which makes the difference, and Savoy managements have succeeded in instilling this attitude into their staff to make it the unique hotel it is today.

The Kitchen and Restaurants

Beneath the elegant ground floor of The Savoy lies a subterranean secret – a unique white-tiled warren of kitchens covering 800 square metres (almost 3000 square feet), operating 24 hours a day to service the hotel's restaurants, private dining rooms, bedrooms and suites.

Every day, the brigade of seventy-five chefs produces around 200 breakfasts, 300 lunches and up to 800 dinners and suppers, to say nothing of room service meals or late night snacks, afternoon teas and canapés and full-scale banquets for private parties.

The Savoy kitchens never sleep. Even overnight, at least a trio of chefs are on duty to satisfy the nocturnal culinary cravings of guests, or to oversee some lengthy cooking procedure; and of course, there is always equipment to be overhauled or cleaned before the morning watch begins at 4 o'clock. Then the comparative night-time calm gives way to a flurry of activity, with ovens being heated for the breakfast croissants and baked goods, stoves being lit for the cooked breakfast orders, and the early morning arrival and checking of deliveries.

At 9 o'clock, the full brigade arrives and the pace quickens. According to classic French practice, the kitchens are run on army lines. Under the overall command of the *Maître chef de cuisine*, six *sous-chefs* act as brigadiers, barking orders at the fourteen *chefs-de-partie*, who in turn keep an eagle eye on their staff of four or five *commis chef* subalterns. Each *sous-chef* is responsible for his or her section, including the larder

(*garde-manger*); butcher; roast and grilled meats (*rôtissier*); fish (*poissonier*); stocks, sauces and soups (*saucier*); hors d'oeuvres and desserts. It is not a *métier* for the lazy. Working split shifts, the chefs start at 8am and most do not finish until 10pm. As the day progresses, the rest of the workforce joins the melée – kitchen porters, pot-washers (*plongeurs*), runners and urgent waiters from every dining area, all on full physical, mental and vocal alert to ensure that meals are served with the precision and perfect timing that Savoy guests expect.

At the vegetable preparation station, a solitary chef embarks on his task of peeling and preparing the day's orders. Today, he will turn 2500 potatoes and slice 700 each of aubergines (eggplant), courgettes (zucchini) and fennel bulbs. At least he, like the butcher, pastry and fish chefs, works in a cool zone. Pity the rôtissier, who swelters in the intense heat of the griddles, grills, deep-fryers and hot ovens of his station. In the cold fish area, two Japanese chefs are preparing exquisite sashimi canapés. For special occasions, chef Matsamura hones his knife to create carved ice sculptures, which are kept alongside the fish in the walk-in chiller until needed. Around the corner, baked canapés and savoury petits fours are being prepared, along with the sandwiches for afternoon tea and room service orders.

At every turn of the maze, there is a different station. Two vast areas are designed solely for plating dishes for the banqueting rooms – one for hot meals, the other for cold dishes. In each, 500 plates are laid out in serried rows, awaiting today's feast. In the hot food area, the plates are stacked four-deep along the surface of The Savoy's oldest oven, a massive cast-iron monster installed by the great Escoffier. Over a century later, it is still in full working order, blasting out powerful heat which reinforces the illusion that those who work in the kitchens have descended into a latter-day incarnation of Dante's Inferno. And yet amid the chaos and cacophany, there is order and control. Two mottos stuck on the kitchen walls sum up the Savoy ethos. One reads:
"Our customer is king

Our product is paramount
The profit will follow"; the other "Remember: For excellence we strive".

Since The Savoy opened in 1899, seventeen Maître chefs have ruled the kitchens. Without doubt, the most famous was the second "emperor", August Escoffier. A giant among chefs, Escoffier was short in stature and had to wear high-heeled shoes to see over the kitchen ranges and work surfaces. Famed as a culinary genius, he created an array of recipes in honour of famous Savoy guests of his time, including Peach Melba for Dame Nellie Melba and *Cuisses de nymphe Aurore* for the Prince of Wales. The sensuous title of this dish (literally "dawn nymph's thighs") concealed the fact that the thighs were, in fact, frogs' legs, at that time regarded by the British as an abomination. Having received the royal seal of approval, however, they immediately became the dish of the year. Escoffier introduced many modern concepts of kitchen management which are still practised at The Savoy today. Unfortunately, the "emperor" also engaged in a number of malpractices for which he was summarily dismissed in 1898.

A long-serving successor was François Latry, whose reign lasted from 1919 until his death in 1942. He was a favourite of the Russian bass Chaliapin, who loved to sit in the kitchen after a performance, chatting and tasting the chef's new take on classic French dishes. Latry was a master of embellishment, and once created a magnificently decorated chocolate Easter egg, which was filled with priceless diamonds and jewels. Until 1940, the Savoy kitchens retained the tradition of employing only male staff. But war brought a chronic shortage of male labour, and Latry broke with tradition to employ the first female apprentice chef in his kitchen. He was also forced to create a semblance of haute cuisine in the face of chronic food shortages and a maximum budget for an entire dinner, including wine, of 5 shillings. His most famous wartime creation was Woolton Pie, a sustaining dish of root vegetables in pastry, which became a staple in almost every household.

Until the arrival of Silvino Trompetto, Savoy Maître chefs had all been French. Despite his Italianate name, Trompetto was born in London, and soon became famous for his very British steak and kidney pie and bread and butter pudding. But his mastery of classical French cuisine also inspired him to create the quintessential *quenelles de brochet* and the famous *truite saumonée en gondole*.

Shortly after Trompetto's retirement, another non-French Maître chef was appointed – German-born Anton Edelmann, whose reign continued for 21 years. Edelmann started as apprentice to Silvino Trompetto at the age of twenty-five and vowed to return as *Maître chef des cuisines* – and eleven years later, he fulfilled his dream. His first major project was to redesign the old kitchens, which had barely changed since Escoffier's time, and to build an additional upstairs kitchen beside the River Restaurant. In 1986, the state-of-the-art kitchens were officially opened by the late Queen Mother, and here to this day the never-ending cycle of work continues, with chefs working around the clock to cope with the demands of The Savoy's numerous restaurants, banqueting suites and private dining rooms.

Dining at The Savoy

No matter where you choose to eat at The Savoy, you can do it in style. You can dance to a live band while you dine in the elegant River Restaurant, with its twin attractions of fine food and spectacular views of the Thames, or luxuriate in the wood-panelled splendour of The Savoy Grill. For over a century, the rich and famous traditionally came to discuss affairs of business or state in the appropriately formal surroundings of the Grill, while enjoying such quintessentially British dishes as steak and kidney or bread and butter pudding, or Scottish smoked salmon hand-carved at the table. Recently refurbished, the Grill now has a more modern, informal feel, and the classic British dishes are prepared with a lighter touch, but the wood panelling and general atmosphere of elegance remain.

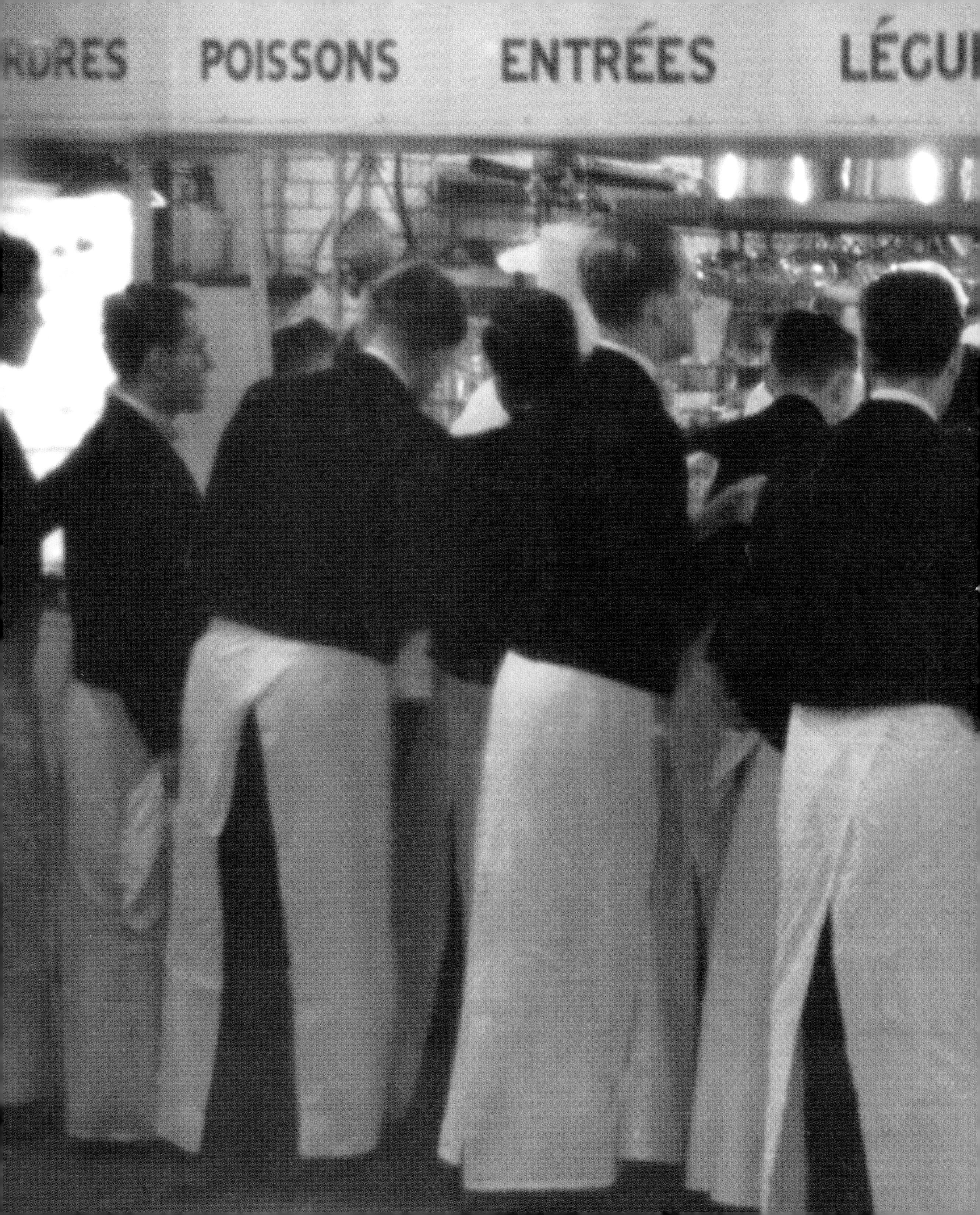
POISSONS
ENTRÉES

There's a touch of the Orient in the Upstairs Restaurant, perched above the hotel's main entrance. Here, a trio of Japanese chefs skilfully prepares fresh sushi and sashimi before your eyes. East and West meet with a fusion of Oriental dishes and great British classics prepared in the subterranean kitchens, including timeless Savoy favourites like kedgeree, lamb cutlets and sticky toffee pudding. Sitting at a window table, enjoying a pre- or post-theatre supper, diners can watch the comings and goings of taxis and luxury cars, choreographed with balletic precision by the liveried doormen, as hotel guests arrive and depart in the courtyard below.

But there's more to Savoy dining than its restaurants alone. Above all, the hotel is famous for its banqueting business. In the course of a year, more than two hundred functions are held, from huge charity banquets to film launches, literary lunches, weddings and intimate private parties. Cocktail nibbles, canapés, multi-course banquets – for all these combined with the regular restaurant orders, the kitchens turn out more than 600,000 meals in a year!

The largest and grandest banqueting suite is the Lancaster Ballroom, an elegant marvel of yellow and gold, lit by crystal chandeliers and wall sconces, which even boasts its own stage and grand piano. This is the place to throw a really swish reception for 800 guests or a swanky dinner for 500 – the ultimate challenge for chefs and waiters. On a smaller scale, the pillared River Room, with its wonderful view over Embankment Gardens to the sweep of the Thames beyond, is the classic venue for weddings, annual company parties and celebrations, complete with balloons and fireworks.

Ranged along a quintessentially Art Deco corridor are the seven private dining rooms, all named after Gilbert and Sullivan operettas. Here, the spirit of G&S lives on – even the china is painted with characters form The Mikado, Iolanthe and The Gondoliers. The largest private room is Pinafore, where in 1911, Winston Churchill founded "The Other Club" for noteworthy figures from the world of politics and the arts. To this day the Club holds its monthly dinners in the wood-panelled room, presided over by a bust of its famous founder. For many years, Kaspar the carved wooden cat (always the fourteenth guest at a party of potentially unlucky thirteen diners) kept Sir Winston company in Pinafore. But Kaspar himself has been unlucky; due to his unfortunate habit of going awol, he now resides under lock and key in the General Manager's office, and is only released when required to do his dining duties. (See his picture on page 90.)

Nearby is Gondoliers, appropriately painted with scenes of Venice, evoking the elegance of the city which inspired the operetta. Mikado naturally has a more exotic flavour, redolent of Japan, with Oriental lamps, a black lacquered screen and delicate Japanese fabrics.

Overlooking the river, Princess Ida and Patience meet to form an elegant room, whose yellow stuccoed walls are graced by a Singer Sargent portrait of a society lady. Perhaps this was where she engaged in her flirtations – who knows? Perhaps she preferred to work her magic in the most intimate private room of all – Sorcerer, a rich red boudoir-like room with damask curtains and upholstery, and a seating capacity of only six. From six to six hundred; from corporate to cosy, The Savoy is the perfect place for a party.

THUR   FRI   SAT

Breakfast

"In order to eat well in England" declared the writer Somerset Maugham, "one must have breakfast three times a day". As Maître Chef des Cuisines at The Savoy you could hardly expect me to agree with that statement – but I do love a traditional English breakfast, although I find it one of the most difficult meals to get right. No two guests, for example, like their eggs cooked in precisely the same way. The American and French visitors can never agree on the perfect breakfast pancake – is a thick pancake with maple syrup better than a thin lacy crêpe with fresh berries? Those in a hurry complain that they wait too long for their morning sustenance, but you cannot produce a freshly cooked breakfast in moments.

A good breakfast needs time both to cook and to enjoy. The Savoy has never served a buffet breakfast; all the dishes are cooked to order. Whether your preference is for a "full English" complete with traditional kedgeree, black pudding (blood sausage), finnan haddock or kippers (smoked herring) – my own favourites – a light "Continental", a healthy "Fitness" menu, or even an authentic Japanese breakfast, it will be freshly prepared in the kitchens with care.

Breakfast preparations begin at 4am. There are always some guests who need nourishment before leaving the hotel for an early flight, and first orders are served in the bedrooms from 5 o'clock. The kitchens are filled with the appetizing aromas of baking croissants, simmering porridge and sizzling bacon, sausages and eggs. Whether Savoy guests choose to have their breakfast in the restaurant or the privacy of their rooms, the chefs are hard at work to make sure that the day gets off to a fine gastronomic start.

Exotic Fruits with Raspberry Coulis

This refreshing fruit ensemble always hits the right spot. You can use any fruits in season provided that they are perfectly ripe to give you maximum enjoyment. We serve this dish for breakfast, but it would also make a perfect appetizer for a light lunch in the summer. Remember you can mix and match to paint your own picture!

SERVES 4

1 mango, peeled and stoned (pitted)
1 papaya, peeled and de-seeded
2 kiwi fruit, peeled
½ pineapple, peeled and cored
½ Charentais or Galia melon, peeled and de-seeded
2 passion fruit
80g/3oz/¾ cup summer berries
  (eg: raspberries, strawberries, blueberries,
  blackberries, loganberries)
4 physalis
200ml/7fl oz/scant 1 cup Raspberry Coulis (see recipe below)
12 tiny mint sprigs

Cut the mango, papaya, kiwi fruit, pineapple and melon into even 3mm/⅛in slices and arrange decoratively on 4 plates.
Cut the passion fruit into quarters and place them between the other fruits; sprinkle the berries over the plate. Peel back the papery leaves of the physalis and put a fruit on each plate.
Drizzle a little raspberry coulis around the fruits and garnish with mint sprigs.

RASPBERRY COULIS

Makes about 300ml/10fl oz/1¼ cups

300g/11oz/scant 2 cups raspberries
2 tsp lemon juice
40g/1½oz/⅓ cup icing (confectioners') sugar

Purée the raspberries in a blender, then add the lemon juice and sugar. Pass through a fine sieve or muslin (cheesecloth).

Smoothies

Smoothies are what many people want for breakfast these days. I often whizz them up at home for my children, who all love them. It's nice to experiment and dream up new combinations, the outcome is often surprising and, more often than not, a winner.

EACH SMOOTHIE SERVES 2

RASPBERRY HEAT WAVE

250g/9oz/1½ cups raspberries
juice of 4 oranges
2 ripe bananas
200ml/7fl oz/scant 1 cup crème fraîche

Whizz all the ingredients in a blender until very smooth.

TROPICAL REVIVER

¼ watermelon, peeled
½ pineapple, peeled and cored
1 mango, peeled and stoned (pitted)
½ banana, peeled
125ml/4fl oz/½ cup natural (plain) yogurt

Juice the watermelon in a juicer, pour into a blender with all the other ingredients and some ice cubes, and whizz until smooth.

ENGLISH CLASSIC

12 strawberries, hulled
2 red apples, peeled and cored
2 pears, peeled and cored
100ml/3½fl oz/scant ½ cup natural (plain) yogurt
2 tsp honey

Put all the ingredients in a blender with some ice cubes, and whizz until smooth.

SPANISH PARADISE

½ Galia or Charentais melon, peeled and de-seeded
3 kiwi fruit
200g/7oz/1¾ cups seedless white grapes
200ml/7fl oz/scant 1 cup natural (plain) yogurt

Put all the ingredients in a blender with some ice cubes, and whizz until smooth.

PLANTER'S DELIGHT

½ pineapple, peeled and cored
½ banana
250ml/9fl oz/generous 1 cup coconut milk
4 tsp grenadine
juice of ½ lemon
a pinch of ground cinnamon

Put all the ingredients in a blender with some ice cubes, and whizz until smooth.

VIRGIN MARY

6 plum tomatoes
2 celery stalks
½ fresh red chilli, de-seeded
½ cucumber
3 carrots
2 tbsp cream cheese
Worcestershire sauce
Tabasco sauce
a small handful of basil leaves
salt and freshly ground pepper

Juice all the vegetables in a juicer, stir in the cream cheese and season to taste with Worcestershire sauce, Tabasco sauce and salt and pepper. Shred the basil and stir in.

EMERALD DREAM

1 ripe avocado, peeled and stoned (pitted)
1 tomato, peeled
200ml/7fl oz/scant 1 cup milk
100ml/3½fl oz/scant ½ cup crème fraîche
Worcestershire sauce, to taste

Put all the ingredients in a blender with some ice cubes, and whizz until smooth.

French Crêpes with Fresh Berries

What a wonderful start to any rainy English day! These superb crêpes are bound to make you smile … right up to lunchtime.

SERVES 4

FOR THE CRÊPES

200g/7oz/1⅔ cups plain (all-purpose) flour
pinch of salt
4 eggs
8 tbsp caster (superfine) sugar
600ml/1pint/2½ cups milk

80g/3oz/6 tbsp unsalted (sweet) butter
400g/14oz/3½ cups mixed berries in season (eg: strawberries, raspberries, blueberries, blackberries, loganberries)
juice and seeds of 4 passion fruit
125ml/4fl oz/½ cup crème fraîche
2 tbsp icing (confectioners') sugar
4 tiny mint sprigs, to garnish

To make the batter: Sift the flour and salt into a large bowl, then add the eggs, caster (superfine) sugar and ¼ of the milk, and mix to a thick batter. Gradually stir in the rest of the milk. The batter should be smooth; if there are any lumps, rub it through a fine sieve.
To cook the crêpes: Melt the butter in a non-stick pan until it begins to froth, then whisk half into the batter. Heat a 20cm/8in non-stick crêpe or frying pan (skillet) and brush it with a little of the remaining butter. Ladle in enough batter to cover the base of the pan in a thin layer, rotating the pan gently to spread the batter evenly. Cook for 30 seconds, then turn the crêpe over and cook for another 30 seconds, until both sides are evenly brown. Continue in this way until all the batter has been used up; you need 16 crêpes. Mix the berries and passion fruit seeds and juice with a little of the crème fraîche; place a spoonful on one corner of each crêpe. Fold it in half, then fold in half again to make a parcel. Put 4 parcels on each plate, dust with icing (confectioners') sugar, and top with a spoonful of crème fraîche. Garnish with a sprig of mint and a few mixed berries.

Fruit Compote with Crème Fraîche

This old time favourite is still a popular breakfast dish at The Savoy. The customers enjoy it because it is good to eat, easy on the stomach and a very healthy way to start the day.

SERVES 4

8 prunes, dried or *mi-cuits*, stoned (pitted)
400ml/14fl oz/1½ cups Stock Syrup (see page 185)
2 apples (eg: Granny Smith), peeled, cored and cut in quarters
2 pears (eg: Comice or Williams), peeled, cored and cut in quarters
2 peaches, peeled, stoned (pitted) and cut in half
2 figs
2 plums, stoned (pitted) and cut in half
4 tbsp (or more) crème fraîche, to serve

If you use dried prunes, soak them for 2–3 hours, changing the water twice.
Heat the syrup in a pan, add the apples, and poach at a simmer for 4–5 minutes until tender. Remove them and poach all the other fruits separately in the same way. When they are all cooked, put them all back in the syrup and leave to cool.
Serve the compote with a generous topping of crème fraîche.

Smoked Haddock and Salmon Kedgeree with Curry Sauce

This classic dish is no longer top of the breakfast pops nowadays, but as a foreigner I feel I have to keep up this British tradition, which I am sure will disappear in my children's generation. I think kedgeree has earned its place in the country's culinary canon, provided that is made with finnan haddie or smoked haddock. This imparts a distinctive flavour to the dish, which can be quite bland without it. The salmon adds contrasting colour and texture. For a richer dish, serve some reduced cream on the side, along with the curry sauce.

SERVES 4

150ml/5fl oz/⅔ cup Chicken Stock
  (see page 180) or water
½ onion, finely chopped
2 tbsp oil
120g/4oz/generous ½ cup long grain rice
150g/5oz undyed smoked haddock (preferably finnan haddie),
  skin and bones removed.
150g/5oz salmon fillets, skin and bones removed
4 hard-boiled (hard-cooked) eggs, peeled
2 tbsp butter
80g/3oz/scant ½ cup peas, cooked
2 tbsp parsley leaves, washed and shredded
300ml/10fl oz/1¼ cups curry sauce (see recipe right)
200ml/7fl oz/scant 1 cup double (heavy) cream, reduced by half
salt

Heat the oven to 180°C/350°F/Gas Mark 4. Heat the chicken stock or water to boiling point and add salt to taste. Put the onion and oil in a large, shallow pan and sweat until soft and translucent. Add the rice and stir until all the grains are coated in the oil. Add the boiling stock or water, and cover with buttered greaseproof (waxed) paper. Cook in the oven for about 20 minutes.
Meanwhile, prepare a steamer, put the fish in the top, and steam for about 4 minutes, until translucent. Take off the heat and cover the fish to stop it drying out.
Chop 2 of the eggs. Break up the fish into large flakes. Remove the rice from the oven and stir in the butter to separate the grains. Add the fish, peas, chopped eggs and 1½ tbsp of the parsley, and stir gently until well mixed. Place the kedgeree in a warm dish. Quarter the remaining eggs and arrange them on top. Sprinkle with the remaining shredded parsley; serve the curry sauce and reduced cream on the side.

CURRY SAUCE

It is not easy to prepare a smaller quantity of this curry sauce, as you won't get a good flavour, but it freezes well, so you can keep some in stock for another time. This is a fruity variety that goes well with kedgeree.

SERVES 10

1 large onion, finely chopped
3 garlic cloves, finely chopped
1 tbsp oil
15g/½oz/1 tbsp butter
2 chillies, de-seeded and chopped
4 tbsp curry powder
1 tsp ground turmeric
2 tbsp tomato purée (paste)
½ apple, cored and chopped
½ banana, sliced
¼ cinnamon stick
1 litre/1¾ pints/4 cups Chicken Stock (see page 180)
salt

In a large pan, sweat the onion and garlic in the oil and butter until soft and translucent. Add the chillies, curry powder and turmeric and sweat for a further minute, then add the tomato purée (paste), apple, banana, cinnamon and chicken stock. Simmer over very low heat for 20 minutes.
Remove the cinnamon stick and process the sauce in a blender. Pass it through a sieve and season with a little salt.

Scrambled Eggs Wrapped in Smoked Salmon

This excellent breakfast or brunch dish may perhaps seem slightly old-fashioned in its presentation, but it sits lightly on the stomach and is always in demand at The Savoy. Don't use smoked salmon with too strong a smoke flavour, as it kills the delicate taste of the scrambled eggs.

SERVES 4

400g/14oz smoked salmon, thinly sliced
12 organic eggs, whisked
20g/¾oz/1½ tbsp unsalted (sweet) butter
2 tbsp double (heavy) cream
15g/½oz/½ cup snipped chives
1 lemon, peeled, all pith removed, cut into rounds
15g/½oz/½ cup chervil leaves, kept in iced water
salt and freshly ground pepper

Heat the grill (broiler). Line 8 ramekins with the slices of smoked salmon, letting them overhang the edges slightly. Season the eggs with salt and pepper.
Heat a non-stick pan, put in the butter, and when it froths, add the eggs and stir with a wooden spoon. When they start to set, take the pan off the heat, add the cream, and keep stirring until they have stopped cooking. Add the chives and fill the lined ramekins with the scrambled eggs. Fold over the overhanging smoked salmon and turn out 2 ramekins on to each plate. Flash the smoked salmon-wrapped eggs under the grill for 30 seconds. Top each one with a slice of lemon and sprinkle with the drained chilled chervil leaves.

Savoy Breakfast Eggs with Caviar and Brioche Soldiers

Like many ordinary citizens, Queen Victoria is said to have enjoyed a plain boiled egg for breakfast every morning – albeit eaten from a gold egg cup with a gold spoon. The Savoy breakfast eggs are far from plain; an organic eggshell is filled with creamy scrambled egg and, in classic Savoy style, topped with oscietra caviar. Brioche "soldiers" complete this very special breakfast.

To cut off the top of a raw egg, you can use cut a special egg-cutter (available from good cook shops). Alternatively, soft-boil the eggs, cut off the tops with a serrated knife and scrape out the insides.

SERVES 4

FOR THE SCRAMBLED EGGS

3 large (extra large) organic eggs
15g/½ oz/1 tbsp unsalted (sweet) butter
2 tbsp double (heavy) cream
4 large (extra large) egg shells, scraped out (see above)
2 tsp oscietra caviar
salt and freshly ground pepper

FOR THE BRIOCHE

(MAKES 1 LOAF OR 20 ROLLS)

15g/½ oz/1 cake fresh yeast
2 tsp caster (superfine) sugar
175 ml/6fl oz/¾ cup milk
500g/1lb 2oz/4 cups strong white bread flour
1 tsp salt
1 large (extra large) egg, beaten with 2 large (extra large) egg yolks
150g/5oz/⅔ cup unsalted (sweet) butter, softened
butter for greasing and flour for dusting
1 egg yolk, lightly beaten, for glazing

First make the brioche: Mix the yeast and sugar to a smooth paste with the milk. Sift the flour and salt into the bowl of an electric mixer, then pour in the yeast mixture and the beaten egg and yolk mixture. Beat until the dough becomes smooth, elastic and shiny. Add the butter, a small piece at a time, and beat until the dough comes away from the sides of the bowl. Shape it into a ball and place in a buttered bowl. Cover with cling film (plastic wrap) and leave to rise in a warm place for 2 hours.

Tip the risen dough out of the bowl on to a floured surface and press your finger into it to deflate it. Put it into a greased 1kg/2lb loaf tin (pan) and cover again. Leave in a warm place for about 45 minutes until well risen.

To make brioche rolls: Divide the dough into 20 pieces and leave to rise as above. Break off small pieces to make the characteristic "heads". Bake for 10 minutes at 230°C/450°F/Gas Mark 8.

To bake: Heat the oven to 200°C/400°F/Gas Mark 6. Brush the risen brioche with beaten egg yolk and bake in the oven for about 40 minutes. Remove it from the tin (pan) and leave to cool on a wire rack.

To make the scrambled eggs: Lightly beat the eggs and season with salt and pepper. Melt the butter in a small non-stick pan and pour in the eggs. Stir slowly until they start to scramble, but are still liquid, then add the cream. Use a teaspoon to fill the eggshells with the scrambled eggs and top with a little caviar. Serve with toasted brioche "soldiers".

Grilled (Broiled) Kippers (Smoked Herring) with Fried Quails' Eggs

I think kippers (smoked herring) are one of life's great treasures. The aroma and flavour of a lightly grilled (broiled) kipper is simply amazing, yet scarcely anyone abroad has heard of them. I sometimes think we should go on a big selling spree to the continent; I am convinced that everyone would absolutely love kippers once they discovered them. This could be my contribution to Britain's payment deficit.

SERVES 4

4 undyed kippers (smoked herring)
50g/2oz/¼ cup butter, softened
4 rashers (slices) of smoked streaky (fatty) bacon, rinds removed,
  cut into 5mm/¼in wide strips
2 slices of white bread, crusts removed, cut into 5mm/¼in cubes
4–8 quails' eggs
4 tsp olive oil
15g/½oz/½ cup flat leaf parsley leaves
freshly ground pepper

Heat the grill (broiler) to high. Rub the kippers (smoked herring) all over with a little butter and grill (broil) them for 5–6 minutes. Meanwhile, put the bacon in a non-stick frying pan (skillet) and cook over high heat until very crispy, then drain through a fine sieve, pouring the fat back into the pan. Using the same bacon fat, fry the bread cubes until crispy and brown.
In another pan, quickly fry the quails' eggs in the remaining butter and the olive oil, and drain on kitchen paper (paper towels). Remove the kippers from under the grill and take the flesh off the bones (it will come off very easily once they are cooked). Place the boned kippers fillets on serving plates. Shred the parsley and mix it with the bacon and bread cubes. Put 1 or 2 quails' eggs on each kipper and sprinkle the bacon and fried bread over and around.

Art Deco at The Savoy

From the start, The Savoy Hotel was the epitome of modern design. Designed by Thomas Collcutt, with interiors by the doyen of art nouveau, Arthur Mackmurdo, it was the last word in innovation.

The first steel-framed building, the first to use concrete, the first to be built around a courtyard (complete with fountain) and to boast its own artesian well, constant hot water, 24-hour electric lights, and state-of-the-art lacquered "ascending rooms" (lifts/elevators) – the whole seven-storey design seemed perfect.

But almost immediately, changes were made to improve it. A new, more ornate fountain replaced the original, and in 1904, the grand new entrance we know today was created in the Strand. Uniquely, traffic was kept on the right, to keep the hotel entrance clear as the audiences arrived at the adjacent theatre. It still remains the only road in Britain where you drive on the right. A statue of Count Peter of Savoy was commissioned to stand above the original stone archway. Nowadays, he stands proudly on the apex of the stainless steel canopy above the "V" of Savoy, welcoming arriving guests. Behind him, above the carved mahogany panelling, is the "new" classical frieze designed by Basil Pegram for the 1904 front hall.

The Paris Exhibition of 1925, showcasing the world's best new designs, changed everything. Art Deco took the world by storm. Suddenly the Edwardian Savoy décor, with its gilded cornices and columns and ornate carved mahogany interior seemed old-fashioned. At the age of thirty-five, the old lady needed a facelift.

After the horrors of the First World War, Art Deco symbolized the limitless possibilities of the future. Combining fantasy and luxury with industrial materials such as metal and glass, the style was streamlined and modern – just what the ageing Savoy needed. When The Savoy Theatre was rebuilt in 1929, an astonished public saw for the first time a façade made from stainless steel (a brand-new material). Then – more revolutionary still – a matching steel canopy was erected above the hotel entrance.

Inside, the walls were panelled in pale wood with simple geometric lines, glamorized with mirrors. Basil Ionides, whose decorative ironwork already adorned the theatre, designed the banisters and ornate rope and tassel balustrades that still exist, as do his state-of-the-art fittings in the luxurious remodelled marble bathrooms. From a single piece of black plane wood, he carved The Savoy's oldest extant resident, Kaspar the 1-metre/3-foot high cat.

Wherever you look at The Savoy, you will find traces of Art Deco. Step back eighty years into the Private Rooms corridor. Here, all the wall coverings, light fittings and door surrounds are the originals dating from the 1920s and 30s. And in the lower Thames foyer, three magnificent mirrors reflecting vast flower-filled vases embody the 1930s perfection of London's most famous Art Deco hotel.

Poached Cinnamon and Orange-scented Figs with Frozen Vanilla Yogurt

Figs are readily available during the summer and when they are very ripe and plump, you need to do very little to create a refreshing breakfast dish, which can also be served as a dessert. This recipe is not only simple but also very quick to make.

SERVES 4

2 vanilla pods (beans), plus extra for garnishing
200ml/7fl oz/scant 1 cup natural (plain) yogurt
12 ripe figs
300ml/10fl oz/1¼ cups Stock Syrup (see page 185)
pinch of saffron threads
2 cinnamon sticks, plus extra for garnishing
2 tbsp ruby port
½ lemon

To make the frozen yogurt: Split and scrape 1 vanilla pod (bean) into the yogurt, stir and place in 4 small freezerproof ramekins and freeze.

Bring the stock syrup and cinnamon to simmering point, split and scrape in the other vanilla pod, and add the port and saffron. Wash the figs, put them in the hot syrup, and simmer for 4–5 minutes. Leave the figs in the syrup and cool to lukewarm. Remove the cooled figs from the syrup and cut a 1cm/½in deep cross in the top of each fig. Place 3 figs on each plate and drizzle the syrup over and around them. Place a piece of frozen yogurt over the figs and decorate with a vanilla pod and piece of cinnamon bark.

Lunch

Lunch is my favourite meal of the day. At The Savoy, it always presents the staff with a challenge, as they have to cater for so many different requirements – long lazy lunches in the River Restaurant; serious business affairs in the Savoy Grill and the eight Private dining and Banqueting rooms; casual light snacks in the Thames Foyer with a 2-course "fast" lunch with a glass of wine for those in a hurry – an omelette Arnold Bennett or tomato tart with goat's cheese, or perhaps some sushi – and of course, the hotel always offers the comfort of Room Service as well. For the customers, lunch begins after midday, but in the kitchens, preparations start at 8.30am. As lunchtime approaches, the atmosphere becomes ever more hectic, as up to 38 chefs execute the orders flying in from every direction.

Every day, a different dish is offered on the table d'hôte menu, using seasonal produce fresh from the market. Some days it's traditional English – roast beef with Yorkshire pudding, sausages and mash with onion gravy, or Shepherd's pie and peas – but if the produce is right, the chefs will create surprising dishes such as seared cod with pig's cheeks on choucroûte with parsley mash, which are hugely popular.

For those with time to spare, weekday lunches are unhurried affairs, with well-dressed ladies enhancing the elegant surroundings. In Escoffier's day, fashionable women frequented The Savoy in large numbers, but nowadays only 25 per cent of the customers are women, a fact I very much regret; I wish there were more "ladies who lunch". But on Saturdays and Sundays, they come with their families to linger over a very relaxed lunch, and I love that. It's great to see people unwind for a few hours in the middle of the day. It makes all the hustle and bustle in the kitchens seem worthwhile.

Marinated Sea Bass and Salmon with Mouli (Daikon) and Wasabi

Throughout the late 1980s and 90s, I used to spend two weeks each January working in Japan – a fantastic place for food lovers. The variety and careful thought the Japanese put into their food is truly astonishing (as are the prices they charge!) This is my adaptation of a dish I ate on the bullet train travelling from Tokyo to Kobe. I was very sceptical about the reception it would get from Savoy customers, but they loved it, and all these years later, it still features on the lunch and private room menus. All the Japanese ingredients are widely available.

SERVES 4

50g/2oz mouli (daikon), peeled and washed
50g/2oz carrot, peeled and washed
50ml/2fl oz/¼ cup Lemon Dressing (see page 182)
2 tsp chilli oil
200g/7oz sea bass fillet, scaled, skin and pin bones removed
  (preferably taken from a wild fish weighing about 2kg/4½ lb)
200g/7oz organic farmed salmon, skin and pin bones removed
1 fresh green chilli
50g/2oz/2 cups fresh coriander (cilantro) leaves, washed
1 tsp ready-mixed wasabi
salt and freshly ground pepper

Cut the mouli (daikon) and carrot into very fine long strips, using a mandoline if you have one. Mix them together. Mix the lemon dressing with the chilli oil.
Trim both fish fillets to make them the same width. Dry them on kitchen paper (paper towels), and place in the freezer for 30 minutes to firm up the flesh. Using a very sharp knife, cut the chilled fillets into 3mm/⅛in thick slices.
Lightly brush the bottom of each serving plate with a little dressing, and grind on some black pepper. Arrange the slices of fish in layers, alternating the sea bass and salmon, and overlapping them slightly. Allow 3 slices of each fish per serving. Brush the top of the fish with more dressing, and again grind a little pepper on top. Place a heap of mouli and carrot in the middle.
Cut the chilli into very fine rings and lay them around the fish. Pour the remaining dressing on top, and garnish with coriander (cilantro) leaves. Spoon a little wasabi on to the edge of the plate, and serve.

Marinated Sardines with Lumpfish "Caviar"

Make sure you use only the very freshest sardines for this recipe, as the success of this simple dish depends entirely on their freshness and quality. For the same reason, you must also choose the best extra virgin olive oil.

SERVES 4

6–8 medium fresh sardines, about 40g/1½ oz each, filleted
300ml/10fl oz/1¼ cups white wine vinegar
50g/2oz/⅓ cup peeled and finely diced carrots
50g/2oz/¼ cup finely diced leek
50g/2oz/⅓ cup peeled and finely diced celeriac (celery root)
40g/1½oz/3 tbsp lumpfish roe
3 ripe plum tomatoes
4 very thin slices of white bread
200ml/7fl oz/scant 1 cup extra virgin olive oil
salt and freshly ground pepper
chervil leaves, to garnish

Wash and dry the sardine fillets. Put them in a non-metallic dish and pour on the white wine vinegar and 600ml/1 pint/2½ cups water. Season with salt and pepper, cover, and leave to marinate in the refrigerator for 12 hours.
Fill a large pan with salted water and bring to the boil.
Plunge in the vegetables and blanch them very quickly, then drain and refresh in iced water. Pat the vegetables dry, and mix with the lumpfish roe.
Blanch the tomatoes in boiling water, peel, de-seed and chop them very finely. Place them in a square of muslin (cheesecloth) and squeeze out the liquid. Cut the thin slices of bread into 5 x 4cm/ 2 x 1½in rectangles, and toast them.
Remove the sardines from their marinade, and dry on kitchen paper (paper towels). Roll them into paupiettes or rollmops. Put 2–3 in each serving bowl, top with the vegetables, and drizzle over some olive oil and a little of the tomato juice. Garnish with chervil; serve the toast on the side.

Salad of Baby Artichokes and Spicy Chicken Winglets with Parmesan Crisps

The robust flavours of the chillies and lemon dressing add complexity to the basic simplicity of this salad appetizer. The recipe also works well without the chicken winglets if you need a speedy vegetarian dish. Just add an extra Parmesan crisp or two. A yogurty raita makes a delicious accompaniment.

SERVES 4

24 chicken winglets

FOR THE MARINADE

200ml/7fl oz/scant1 cup natural (plain) yogurt
1 fresh red chilli, de-seeded and finely chopped
2 garlic cloves, crushed
½ tsp cayenne pepper
1 tsp chopped fresh root ginger
8 baby artichokes (peeled)
juice of ½ lemon
8 cherry tomatoes, halved
1½ tbsp freshly grated Parmesan cheese
80g/3oz/1½ cups wild rocket
4 tbsp Lemon Dressing (see page 182)
oil, for deep-frying
salt and freshly ground pepper
4 Parmesan crisps (see recipe right)

To prepare the chicken winglets: Peel back the skin on the thin end of the winglets and push back the meat, exposing both bones down to the knuckle. Remove the thin bone with a sharp knife.
Mix the yogurt with the chilli, garlic, cayenne and ginger, add the winglets and mix well. Cover and marinate in the refrigerator for at least 2 hours.

Remove the straggly outer leaves from the baby artichokes, and trim the stalk to about 4cm/1½in. Boil in salted water with the lemon juice for about 15 minutes until tender, and leave to cool in the cooking liquid. When cold, drain the artichokes and dry on a double thickness of kitchen paper (paper towels). Cut them in half and remove the woolly choke inside.
Heat the grill (broiler) to high. Season the cherry tomatoes with salt and pepper, sprinkle with a little Parmesan, and grill (broil) until the cheese is lightly browned and bubbly.
Heat the oven to 200°C/400° F/Gas Mark 6.
To cook the chicken winglets: Heat the oil to 160°C/320°F. Meanwhile, take the winglets out of the yogurt marinade, and pat dry. Fry the winglets in the hot oil until brown and crispy. You will need to check carefully that they are thoroughly cooked, as they take longer than you might think. If they are well browned, but not cooked through, put them in the hot oven and bake for 5–10 minutes until fully cooked.
To serve: Place the cherry tomatoes and artichokes on individual plates. Toss the rocket in the lemon dressing, divide it among the plates, top each salad with a Parmesan crisp and arrange the chicken winglets around it.

PARMESAN CRISPS

MAKES 4

40g/1½oz/½ cup freshly grated Parmesan cheese

Heat the oven to 200°C/400°F/Gas Mark 6. Place a round 5–6cm/2–2¼ in pastry (cookie) cutter on a baking tray (cookie sheet) lined with non-stick parchment, and sprinkle in a quarter of the Parmesan. Lift off the cutter and repeat to make 3 more rounds. Bake in the oven for 3–5 minutes until bubbly and melted, then remove and leave to cool.
For an interesting variation, sprinkle 2 tbsp poppy seeds over the crisps before baking.

Polenta Crisps with Guacamole and Tofu (Beancurd)

This is an old and very reliable stalwart at The Savoy, much enjoyed by vegetarian customers. To ring the changes, I sometimes use smoked tofu (beancurd), which adds a deliciously different flavour. If you are not a vegetarian, but like the idea of this dish, add some well-drained cubes of poached or smoked fish or smoked chicken to the guacamole.

SERVES 4

1 litre/1¾ pint/4 cups Vegetable Stock (see page 182)
350g/12oz/scant 2½ cups polenta
2 tbsp mixed fresh herbs (flat parsley, tarragon, chives)
40g/1½ oz/½ cup freshly grated Parmesan cheese
salt

FOR THE GUACAMOLE

1 ripe avocado
¼ garlic clove, crushed
½ red onion, finely chopped
2 spring onions (scallions), trimmed and thinly sliced
2 plum tomatoes, peeled, de-seeded and diced
juice of ½ lemon
½ tsp Tabasco sauce
pinch of ground cumin
pinch of cayenne pepper or chilli powder
celery salt and freshly ground pepper

FOR THE GARNISH

oil, for deep-frying
2 shallots, sliced into thin rings
400ml/14fl oz/1¾ cups milk
2 tsp plain (all-purpose) flour
1 tsp sweet paprika
2 tbsp olive oil
200g/7oz tofu (beancurd), diced
80g/3oz/1½ cups Herb Salad (see page 95)
4 tsp Lemon Dressing (see page 182)

In a large pan, bring the stock to the boil, add a large pinch of salt, then whisk in the polenta in a steady stream. Push the pan to one side and cook over indirect heat for about 20 minutes, stirring constantly, until the polenta is very smooth and well thickened. Stir in the herbs and Parmesan, then pour the polenta evenly on to a tray 1cm/½in deep. Cool and chill until well set, then cut into 12 rounds with a 7cm/2¾in pastry (cookie) cutter.

To make the guacamole: Peel the avocado, remove the stone (pit), and cut the flesh into small cubes. Add all the other ingredients and mix well. (You can prepare the guacamole in advance, but be sure to keep the stone in the avocado to avoid discoloration.)
To prepare the garnish: In a deep-fat fryer or deep pan, heat the olive oil to 160°C/320°F. Dip the shallot rings into the milk and then the flour mixed with the paprika. Shake off the excess, and deep-fry the shallots until golden brown. Drain and keep warm.
To assemble the dish: Heat the oven to 180°C/350°F/ Gas Mark 4. Heat the olive oil in a non-stick frying pan (skillet), and fry the polenta rounds until coloured on both sides. Place 4 rounds on a baking tray (cookie sheet), put a 5mm/¼in layer of guacamole and some diced tofu (beancurd) on each one, then place another round on top and make a second layer of guacamole and tofu. Top this with a final polenta round. Heat the assembled polenta crisps in the oven for 5 minutes, then place one in the centre of each plate. Top with a little more guacamole, and garnish with the shallot rings.
Toss the herb salad in the lemon dressing and arrange the salad around the polenta crisps.

Spring Roll of Confit Rabbit Legs and Morels with Plum Dressing

The sweetness of the rabbit and the smoothness of the mango work well together, and the combination of the soft filling wrapped in a crunchy packaging makes this a memorable lunch appetizer, which always goes down well with our customers.

SERVES 4

50g/2oz fresh or dried morels
 (get the small ones as they are much nicer)
300ml/10fl oz/1¼ cups extra virgin olive oil
pinch of saffron threads
8 sheets of brik or filo pastry
1 egg, beaten
2 Confit Rabbit Legs, flaked (see page 116)
200g/7oz mixed vegetables (carrots, onions, celery, leek),
 cut into 5mm/¼ in dice, and blanched
1 shallot, chopped
100g/3½oz/½ cup Plum Chutney (see page 182)
1 mango peeled, stoned (pitted) and cut into 1cm/½ in wide strips
oil, for deep-frying
2 tomatoes, peeled, de-seeded and diced
juice of ½ lemon

If you are using dried morels, soak them for 2 hours, changing the water twice. Trim off the stalks and wash thoroughly.
To make the saffron oil: Warm the olive oil and add the saffron. Leave to infuse (steep) for 20 minutes, pass through a sieve and reserve.
To make the spring rolls: Lay out 1 sheet of brik or filo pastry and brush with beaten egg. Top with another sheet and brush the edges with the egg. Mix the flaked rabbit legs with two-thirds of the diced vegetables, the chopped shallot, and two-thirds of the plum chutney. Spread a 12 x 2cm/4¾ x ¾in strip of the rabbit mixture diagonally across the centre of the pastry, from one corner to the other, leaving about 3cm/1in at the ends; arrange some mango on top. Fold the 4 corners into the centre and roll into a cylinder. Make 3 more spring rolls in this way.
Heat the deep-frying oil to 160°C/320°F and fry the spring rolls for about 4 minutes until golden brown. Drain on kitchen paper (paper towels).
Mix the remaining diced vegetables and the diced tomatoes with the morels. Mix the saffron oil with the rest of the plum chutney and the lemon juice and add one-third of this mixture to the vegetable and morel mixture.
To serve: Cut each spring roll into 2 cylinders at an angle and arrange on the plates. Garnish with the vegetables and morels and sprinkle the remaining plum and saffron oil around the edge.

Grilled (Broiled) Mackerel in Smoked Bacon on Grilled (Broiled) Rustic Tomato Bread

Make sure that your mackerel is very fresh and that you have removed all the bones. Bacon and mackerel are a classic pairing; the bacon helps to bring out the rich flavour of the fish. For a light lunch dish in its own right, serve two mackerel fillets per person.

SERVES 4

4 tbsp olive oil
juice of ½ lemon
4 very ripe vine tomatoes
4 slices of rustic (sourdough) bread
2 garlic cloves, crushed
4 x 80g/3oz mackerel fillets, all bones removed
4 very thin rashers (slices) of smoked streaky (fatty) bacon
80g/3oz mixed lettuce leaves
1 bunch of watercress, trimmed and washed
4 tsp Lemon Dressing (see page 182)
sea salt and freshly ground black pepper

Heat the grill (broiler) to high. Mix the olive oil with the lemon juice, and season with salt and pepper to make a dressing.
Crush the tomatoes with the back of a fork until very mushy. Grill (broil) the bread on both sides, and scrape on the garlic, then the crushed tomatoes.
Wrap each mackerel fillet in a bacon rasher (slice) and grill quickly on both sides until just cooked.
Place a fillet on each slice of tomato bread, toss the lettuce and watercress in a little of the lemon dressing, place a little heap beside the mackerel, and serve.

Savoy Dressed Crab

This ever-popular Savoy classic has been copied many times, but in my opinion, the version we serve in The Savoy has never been bettered. It is simple, unfussy and made with the very best and freshest Devon crab. The ingredients speak for themselves.

SERVES 4

200g/7oz white crab meat, all cartilage removed
125 ml/4fl oz/½ cup crème fraîche
200ml/7fl oz/scant 1 cup Mayonnaise (see page 183)
80g/3oz cucumber, peeled, de-seeded and cut into 5mm/¼in dice
1 tbsp mint leaves, shredded
4 tomatoes (about 200g/7oz), peeled, de-seeded and cut into 1cm/½in dice
½ chilli, de-seeded and very finely chopped
20g/¾oz/¾ cup flat leaf parsley leaves, washed and shredded
4 Parmesan and Poppy Seed Crisps (see page 38)
salt and freshly ground pepper

Mix the white crab meat with half the crème fraîche and one-third of the mayonnaise, and season with salt and pepper. Mix the cucumber, mint and half the diced tomatoes with the chilli and the remaining crème fraîche. Mix the remaining mayonnaise with the shredded parsley.

To assemble the dressed crab: Arrange the remaining diced tomatoes in a 10cm/4in pastry ring in the centre of each plate and spread in a little of the mayonnaise mixture. Then place a deep 7cm/2¾in pastry (cookie) cutter in the middle and fill it two-thirds full with the cucumber mix. Top with the crab meat to fill up the pastry cutter. Lift off the cutter and garnish each plate with a Parmesan and poppy seed crisp.

Butternut Squash Tortellini with Wild Mushrooms

This is a combination made in heaven; the sweetness of the squash and the amaretti are in perfect harmony.

SERVES 4

50g/2oz/¼ cup finely chopped onion
2 tbsp oil
1 garlic clove, crushed
4 small or 2 large butternut squash, peeled and cut into small pieces
120g/4oz amaretti
salt and freshly ground pepper

FOR THE PASTA DOUGH

500g/3½ cups flour (Italian tipo 00 pasta flour if possible)
1 tsp salt
2 tsp olive oil
2 eggs
9 egg yolks
pinch of saffron threads mixed with 2 tbsp water, boiled and reduced, then passed through a fine sieve (optional)
eggwash (1 egg yolk mixed with 1 tbsp milk)

FOR THE GARNISH

120g/4oz mixed wild mushroom (eg: girolles, black trumpets, chanterelles, ceps)
120g/4oz/½ cup unsalted (sweet) butter
6 cherry tomatoes
50g/2oz/⅔ cup freshly grated Parmesan cheese
12 sage leaves

To make the filling: Sweat the onion in the oil until soft and translucent, then add the garlic and sweat for another minute. Add the butternut squash, sweat gently until very soft, then add the amaretti. Cool and purée in a food processor. Season with salt and pepper.

To make the pasta dough: In a strong food processor, or by hand, combine the flour, salt, olive oil, eggs, yolks and a little saffron reduction if you wish, and process until it becomes a very smooth dough. Wrap it in cling film (plastic wrap) and leave to rest in the refrigerator for at least 30 minutes.

To make the tortellini: Roll out the dough as thinly as possible in a pasta machine (or if necessary by hand), then cut it into 5cm/2in squares (you should make about 20–24 squares). Place 2 tsp of the filling in the middle of each square, and brush the edges with a little eggwash. Fold the pasta squares from corner to corner to make a triangle, then turn the pointed ends inwards, and press them together.

Heat the grill (broiler). Cut the cherry tomatoes in half and sprinkle with the half the Parmesan. Grill (broil) until they are soft and lightly browned.

Cook the tortellini in plenty of boiling salted water for about 3 minutes until cooked. Drain, refresh under cold water, then toss them in a little melted butter, and season with salt and pepper.

To serve: Divide the tomatoes and tortellini among 4 deep soup plates (allow 5 or 6 tortellini per person), sprinkle with the remaining Parmesan, and flash quickly under the hot grill (broiler). Heat the mushrooms and scatter them on top.

In a small pan, heat the remaining butter with the sage leaves. As soon as the butter begins to brown, spoon it and the sage over the tortellini, and serve.

Savoy Game Parcels

I use the mascarpone in these little parcels as a contrast to the strong flavour of the game and a means of mellowing it. Needless to say, Savoy cabbage is the only wrapping to use at The Savoy!

SERVES 4

½ large onion, chopped
2 tbsp olive oil
2 garlic cloves, crushed
40g/1½oz stale white bread, crusts removed
80g/3oz venison shoulder or leg
80g/3oz shoulder of pork
40g/1½oz calves' or duck liver
40g/1½oz/scant ¼ cup mascarpone cheese
1 egg
4 Savoy cabbage leaves, blanched and dried
125ml/4fl oz/½ cup Veal Jus (see page 181)
½ onion, thinly sliced
salt and freshly ground pepper

FOR THE GARNISH

vegetable oil, for deep-frying
3 tbsp plain (all-purpose) flour
1 tbsp paprika
2 shallots, cut into thin rings
125ml/4fl oz/½ cup milk
280g/10oz/3⅓ cups Olive Oil Potato Purée (see page 188)

Heat the oven to 180°C/350°F/Gas Mark 4.

To make the stuffing: In a frying pan (skillet), sweat the chopped onion in 1 tbsp oil until soft and translucent, add the garlic and sweat for another minute. Leave to cool. Soak the bread in a little water and squeeze dry.

Finely mince (grind) the venison, pork, liver and bread, together with the onions and garlic, or finely chop them in a food processor. Add the mascarpone and egg, season with salt and pepper, and mix well. Form into 8 equal balls (about 35g/1¼oz each).

Cut out the thick ribs from the cabbage leaves and cut each leaf in half. Wrap each ball in a cabbage leaf to make a parcel, then wrap in cling film (plastic wrap). Heat the veal jus in a wide pan and put in the cabbage parcels. Cover with a lid and braise slowly in the oven for about 30 minutes. Remove (reserve the jus) and keep warm.

To make the onion gravy: Sweat the sliced onion in the remaining oil until soft and translucent. Add the reserved veal jus and simmer until slightly thickened.

For the garnish: Heat the vegetable oil to 160°C/320°F in a deep-fryer or pan. Mix together the flour and paprika, dip the shallot rings in milk and then the flour mixture. Shake off the excess flour and fry the shallots in the hot oil until brown and crispy. Drain and keep warm. This can be done well in advance.

Divide the olive oil potato purée among 4 warmed plates, unwrap the cabbage parcels and place them on the potato. Spoon over some onion gravy, and garnish with the deep-fried shallots.

Caesar Salad with Hickory-smoked Organic Salmon and Focaccia Croûtons

There is no doubt that the practice of farming salmon, which started in the 1970s, saved the wild salmon from extinction. Wild salmon is a real treat; it is lovely to cook with, and has an amazing flavour, but it is still quite scarce, so stocks should be preserved. Organic farmed salmon is a good way forward. It is not quite as brilliant as its wild relative, but under the circumstances, it is the best alternative. I love it in this light lunch dish.

SERVES 4

500g/18oz hickory wood shavings
4 x 140g/4½ oz organic salmon fillets, pin bones removed
¼ loaf of focaccia, very thinly sliced
2 Cos (romaine) lettuces, outside leaves removed, cut into
  5cm/2in long pieces, washed and dried

FOR THE CAESAR DRESSING

3 egg yolks
1 garlic clove, crushed
2 anchovy fillets
2 tbsp finely chopped shallot
1 tbsp English (hot) mustard
1 tbsp Worcestershire sauce
2 tbsp balsamic vinegar
½ fresh red chilli, de-seeded and finely chopped
125ml/4fl oz/½ cup olive oil
salt and freshly ground pepper

Prepare a smoker with the hickory shavings, put in the salmon fillets, and smoke for 5 minutes, until lightly smoked and cooked medium. Alternatively, if you haven't got a smoker, place the shavings in a small roasting tray (pan) in an oven, set light to them, and heat the oven to 160°C/320°F/Gas Mark 3. Put the salmon on an ovenproof dish and place it next to the shavings. Smoke in the oven for 5 minutes.
To make the croûtons: Decrease the oven temperature to 80°C/175°F or the lowest gas setting. Put in the focaccia slices and leave for 2 hours to dry.
To make the dressing: Combine the egg yolks, garlic, anchovy fillets, shallot, mustard, Worcestershire sauce, balsamic vinegar and chilli in a blender, and process to a purée. With the motor running, gradually pour in the olive oil to make a thick dressing. Season with salt and pepper.
To serve: Toss the lettuce in the dressing and place in a bowl. Top with the salmon and garnish with the dried focaccia croûtons.

Stuffed Courgette (Zucchini) Flowers with Spicy Vegetable Sauce

For sheer presentation you can't beat a courgette (zucchini) flower. In this lovely light vegetarian recipe, gently steaming the flower enhances the depth of colour and the slick of melted butter adds a beautiful sheen. The best flowers come from your own back garden if you are lucky enough to grow courgettes (zucchini). We lesser mortals have to make do with those we can buy in the shops. The spicy vegetable sauce can be used for many different dishes; if you are cooking for non-vegetarians and can use chicken stock instead of vegetable stock, it makes an excellent accompaniment for chicken and even fish dishes.

SERVES 4

FOR THE VEGETABLE SAUCE

1 onion, chopped
2 tbsp oil
1½ red (bell) peppers, de-seeded and finely diced
2 apples, peeled, cored and chopped
pinch of curry powder
pinch of saffron threads
300ml/10fl oz/1¼ cups Vegetable Stock (see page 182)
salt and freshly ground pepper

FOR THE STUFFING

150g/5oz/1 cup grated carrots
100g/3½oz/scant ½ cup butter
70g/3oz potatoes, boiled and passed through a ricer
40g/1½oz/⅓ cup grated Gruyère cheese
1 egg, beaten
4 large courgette (zucchini) flowers, stems removed

FOR THE GARNISH

100g/3½oz baby courgettes (zucchini)
100g/3½oz carrots, sliced and blanched
100g/3½oz/¾ cup broad (fava) beans, skinned
4 tomatoes, peeled, de-seeded and cut into small squares

Put the onion and oil in a pan, cover, and sweat until soft and translucent. Add the diced red (bell) pepper and sweat until soft, then add the apples, curry powder, saffron and vegetable stock. Simmer until all ingredients are soft, transfer to a blender or food processor, and process to a purée. Pass the sauce through a fine sieve and season with salt and pepper.

To stuff the courgette (zucchini) flowers: Sweat the grated carrots in a little butter until soft, remove from the heat and mix with the riced potato and the Gruyère. Add the egg and season with salt and pepper. Fill a piping (pastry) bag with this mixture and pipe it into the courgette flowers.

Prepare a steamer and steam the stuffed flowers for 8 minutes. Melt 25g/1oz/2 tbsp of the remaining butter. Take the flowers out of the steamer and brush with a little melted butter.

To serve: Toss the baby courgettes (zucchini), sliced carrots and broad (fava) beans in the remaining butter, season with salt and pepper, and add the tomatoes. Spread the vegetables over the plates, place a courgette flower on top, and pour the sauce around it.

Tomato Tarts with Glazed Goat's Cheese and Radish Salad

This is a very tasty, quick and easy to cook dish, which I created to satisfy vegetarian customers. The truffle oil and hot goat's cheese really bring out the flavour of the tomatoes. To make the oil mix, always use one part truffle oil to nine parts olive oil, otherwise the truffle oil will overpower the other ingredients

MAKES 4 INDIVIDUAL TARTS

200ml/7fl oz/scant 1 cup olive oil
2 thyme sprigs
2 rosemary sprigs
2 garlic cloves, unpeeled
2 small hard goat's cheese, 80g/3oz each (eg: crottin de Chavignol or Golden Cross), halved horizontally
100g/3½oz Puff Pastry, preferably home-made (see page 186) or top quality bought pastry
1 egg white
8 plum tomatoes
a little truffle oil mix (1 part truffle oil to 9 parts olive oil)
juice of ½ lime
4 tbsp Radish Salad (see page 188)
2 tsp Basil Oil (see page 182)
1 tsp balsamic vinegar
salt and freshly ground pepper

Mix the olive oil, thyme, rosemary and garlic in a dish, put in the goat's cheese, cover and marinate in the refrigerator overnight. Take out the cheese and pat dry. Strain the marinade and reserve. Roll out the pastry to about 5mm/¼ in thick. Using a 14cm/5½ in pastry (cookie) cutter, cut it into 4 rounds. Prick them all over with a fork and leave to rest in the refrigerator for at least 20 minutes. Heat the oven to 220°C/425°F/Gas Mark 7. Brush the pastry rounds with egg white to stop it from going soggy during cooking. Slice the tomatoes and arrange them in a neat ring on top of the pastry rounds, then season with salt and pepper. Bake in the oven for about 20 minutes, until the bases are crusty.
Heat the grill (broiler). Place the goat's cheeses under the hot grill until lightly browned and heated through (check to make sure: the cheese often looks very brown, but it is not hot inside; if necessary, place it in the oven for a few minutes to heat through).
Remove the tarts from the oven, brush lightly with the truffle oil mix and top each one with half a goat's cheese.
Mix the lime juice with the reserved oil from the marinade, and season with salt and pepper. Toss the radish salad in this dressing, and arrange a spoonful on top of each goat's cheese. Drizzle a little basil oil and balsamic vinegar around the tarts, and serve.

Grilled(Broiled) Turbot with Red Wine Reduction and Silver Onions

This lovely dish is perfect for a special lunch, accompanied by a good claret (Bordeaux wine). The wonderful fleshy turbot and the mild acidity of the sauce reduction make a great combination. As turbot is very expensive and quite scarce, you could use halibut instead (although of course it is not quite the same thing). Another alternative is the slender brill; because it is a less meaty fish, you would need to use a fillet without the bone.

SERVES 4

20 small button (pearl) onions
125ml/4fl oz/½ cup olive oil
400ml/14fl oz/1¾ cups red wine
1 tsp redcurrant jelly
200g/7oz/scant 1 cup unsalted (sweet) butter
cayenne pepper
½ lemon
4 turbot steaks on the bone, at least 225g/8oz each
8 basil leaves
40g/1½oz/¾ cup Herb Sauce (see page 95)
125ml/4fl oz/½ cup Lemon Dressing (see page 182)
sea salt and freshly ground pepper

Peel the onions (you must do this at the last moment, or they will form a hard skin during cooking). Put them in a wide pan with half the olive oil; they should be in a single layer but quite tightly packed. Cook over a high heat, turning the onions until they are evenly browned all over. Cover the pan with a lid, turn the heat down very low, and sweat the onions until very soft.
Boil the red wine to reduce it to a thick syrup, then add the redcurrant jelly. Turn off the heat and whisk in the butter. Season with salt, cayenne pepper and a squeeze of lemon. Pass the sauce through a fine sieve and keep it warm, but do not let it boil again.
Heat the oven to 200°C/400°F/Gas Mark 6. Season the fish with salt and pepper. Heat a ridged griddle pan until very hot, add the remaining olive oil, and sear the turbot on both sides. Transfer the fish to a baking tray (cookie sheet), and cook in the hot oven for 6 minutes. Halve the fish steaks, cut along the central bones with a sharp knife and remove them.
Place the basil leaves on one half of the fish steaks and lay the other half of the fish on top. Place a fish steak on each plate, pour a little of the red wine sauce around, and garnish with the onions. Toss the herb sauce in the lemon dressing, pile it on top of the fish, and serve.

Savoy Fish Pie

Fish pie is one of my all-time favourite English dishes and is always popular at lunchtime at The Savoy. I have come up with many variations over the years; this is an innovative version. The addition of smelt eggs is really unusual. If they are hard to find, use soft herring roes instead.

SERVES 4

100g/3½oz mixed leek, celery and carrot, cut into strips
40g/1½ oz/3 tbsp butter
100ml/3½ fl oz/½ cup dry white wine
200ml/7fl oz/ scant 1 cup Fish Stock (see page 180) or
  Chicken Stock (see page 180)
160g/5½ oz organic salmon fillet, skinned and cut into
  2cm/¾ in cubes
160g/5½ oz halibut fillet, skinned and cut into 2cm/¾ in cubes
80g/3oz tiger prawns (jumbo shrimp), halved horizontally
80g/3oz scallops (preferably diver-caught), halved horizontally
80g/3oz cooked lobster meat, cut into 2cm/¾ in cubes
200ml/7fl oz/scant 1 cup double (heavy) cream
40g/1½oz smelt eggs
2 tbsp sesame seeds
salt, freshly ground pepper and cayenne pepper

FOR THE MASH

400g/14oz potatoes (preferably Maris Piper), peeled
3 garlic cloves, peeled
125ml/4fl oz/½ cup double (heavy) cream
50g/2oz/½ cup grated Cheddar cheese
100ml/3½fl oz/scant ½ cup olive oil

To make the mash: Cut the potatoes into even cubes, wash in cold water and drain. Place in a pan, cover with cold water, and add the garlic and salt to taste. Bring to the boil and simmer until the potatoes are tender but not disintegrating. Drain, return the potatoes to the pan and dry over low heat.
Warm the cream. Pass the potatoes through a very fine sieve or potato ricer into a pan. Set over a low heat, add the warm cream, grated cheese, olive oil, salt and pepper. Stir well and keep the mash warm.
To make the fish pie mixture: Heat the oven to 200°C/400°F/Gas Mark 6. In a large pan, sweat the vegetables in the butter until soft, add the white wine and reduce by half. Add the fish or chicken stock and season with a little salt and pepper. Season all the fish and seafood with salt, pepper and a little cayenne. Add the tiger prawns (jumbo shrimp) to the pan and simmer for 1 minute. Add all the other fish and shellfish, and simmer for 30 seconds. Remove all the fish and shellfish with a slotted spoon and cover with cling film (plastic wrap) so that the steam cannot escape.
Reduce the cooking liquid by two-thirds, then add the cream and reduce by half. Put all the fish and seafood into this sauce and season. Add the smelt eggs. Put the pie mixture into a pie dish and pipe the mash on top (if you are feeling creative, you could pipe an attractive fish shape). Sprinkle with the sesame seeds and bake in the oven for 12 minutes. Serve piping hot.

Breast of Free Range Chicken filled with Taleggio and Pancetta on White Chilli Bean Stew

The robust Italianate flavours of the pancetta with the taleggio and the truffle-scented bean stew work wonderfully well together in this hearty winter lunch dish, which makes a meal in itself and requires a good appetite!

SERVES 4

400g/14oz pancetta
160g/5½ oz/generous ¾ cup white haricot (navy) beans,
  soaked in cold water for at least 3 hours
2 onions, finely chopped
2 tbsp olive oil, plus extra for the chicken
3 garlic cloves, crushed
1 fresh red chilli, de-seeded and finely chopped
1 litre/1¾ pints/4 cups Chicken Stock (see page 180)
120g/4oz taleggio cheese, rind removed
4 free range chicken breast portions (150g/5oz each), unskinned
2 tsp truffle oil
15g/½oz/½ cup flat parsley leaves, washed and shredded
salt and freshly ground pepper

To dry the pancetta: Heat the oven to 70°C/150°F or to the lowest gas setting. Cut 4 very thin slices of pancetta and place on a baking tray (cookie sheet) between 2 layers of greaseproof (waxed) paper. Place a flat utensil on top to keep the pancetta flat, and place in the oven for 3 hours until completely dry.

To make the bean stew: Drain the beans and rinse in cold water. In a pan, sweat the onions in 2 tbsp olive oil until soft and translucent, add the garlic and chilli, and sweat for another minute. Add the beans, half the stock and the remaining pancetta (in one piece), and simmer at the lowest possible temperature (or on a heat diffuser) for about 1½ hours until the beans are soft. The beans must always be covered with the stock, so if they absorb it all, keep topping up with more stock. Remove the pancetta, cut it into small squares. Dice the taleggio and mix it with the pancetta.

To stuff the chicken breast portions: Heat the oven to 140°C/ 275°F/Gas Mark 1. Starting at the thick end, use a long, thin knife to cut a long pocket in each chicken portion. Fill with the cheese and pancetta mixture. Heat a little olive oil in a pan and seal the chicken portions (skin side down) until lightly golden. Transfer to a baking tray. Season the chicken with salt and pepper and cook in the oven for 20 minutes.

To serve: Season the beans with salt and pepper, add the truffle oil and parsley, and divide the stew among 4 large soup bowls. Top with the chicken portions and put 2 slices of the dried pancetta on top.

Parmesan-crusted Veal Holstein

This is my adaptation of a classic dish which I have always enjoyed eating. Without wishing to be immodest, I think my new version tastes and looks better than the original. At The Savoy, it often features on the dinner menu, but it is equally suitable for lunch. The veal medallions must be sliced very thinly; ask the butcher to do this for you. When using balsamic vinegar always use one that is thick and aged for at least 8 years. If this is hard to find, buy a thinner balsamic vinegar, reduce it by half and thicken with a little cornflour (cornstarch).

SERVES 4

6 tbsp fresh white breadcrumbs
3 tbsp freshly grated Parmesan cheese
2 tbsp plain (all-purpose) flour
2 eggs, beaten
4 x 120g/4oz medallions of veal cut from the loin, trimmed of all fat
100ml/3½fl oz/scant ½ cup olive oil
350g/12oz spinach leaves, washed, blanched, refreshed and
  squeezed dry
1 tbsp sesame seeds, toasted
4–8 quails' eggs
16 polenta nuggets (see recipe right)
salt and freshly ground pepper

FOR THE GARNISH

4 anchovies, halved lengthways
12 caper berries
100ml/4fl oz/⅔ cup Basil Oil (see page 182)
3 tbsp thick balsamic vinegar (see introduction above)
40g/1½oz/⅓ cup pine nuts, toasted

To cook the veal medallions: Mix the breadcrumbs with the Parmesan and season with salt and pepper. Put this mixture in one flat dish, the flour in another, and the eggs in a third. Turn the veal first in the flour, then in the egg and lastly in the breadcrumb and Parmesan mixture to coat it evenly. Shake off the excess breadcrumbs, then pan-fry the medallions in 2 tbsp olive oil until golden brown on both sides. Keep warm.
Heat the spinach with the sesame seeds and season with salt and pepper. Keep warm.
To fry the eggs: Smear a film of olive oil over a non-stick frying pan (skillet) and put in a 7cm/2¾in pastry (cookie) cutter. Break 2 quails' eggs into the cutter and fry gently until done to your liking. Repeat with the other quails' eggs, frying them 2 at a time.

Fry the polenta nuggets in a non-stick frying pan (skillet) with a little olive oil until golden brown. Divide the spinach between the plates. Place a veal medallion on the spinach, top each one with 1–2 quails' eggs, and garnish with anchovies and caper berries. Arrange the polenta nuggets around the edge.
Mix the basil oil with the balsamic vinegar and drizzle around the plate. Sprinkle with toasted pine nuts and serve.

POLENTA NUGGETS

SERVES 4

500ml/18fl oz/4 cups Chicken Stock (see page 180)
150g/5oz/1 cup polenta
30g/1oz/2 tbsp unsalted (sweet) butter
pinch of freshly grated nutmeg
salt and freshly ground pepper
olive oil or unsalted (sweet) butter, for frying

In a pan, bring the chicken stock to the boil. Whisk in the polenta in a thin steady stream. Cook for 4–6 minutes until thick, whisking continuously. Whisk in the butter and season to taste with nutmeg, salt and pepper. Pour the polenta into a shallow roasting pan, about 24 x 20cm/10 x 8in, to make a layer about 2cm/¾in thick. Leave until cold and set, then cut the polenta into any shape you like. Before serving, fry in hot olive oil or unsalted (sweet) butter until golden brown on both sides.

Quails with Corn Stuffing on Cardamom-flavoured Sweet Potato Rösti

The secret of this dish is in the stuffing; take your time to prepare it and you will be richly rewarded. Boning quails is a time-consuming activity, so make sure that you buy them ready boned; a friendly butcher will do this for you. The cauliflower cream is a very versatile sauce which goes well with almost all vegetables and can be prepared in advance.

SERVES 4

1 onion, finely chopped
2 tbsp oil
1 garlic clove, crushed
125ml/4fl oz/½ cup milk
1 stale white bread roll, cut into thin slices
250g/9oz pork shoulder, rind removed
80g/3oz chicken livers, trimmed
1 egg, plus 1 egg yolk
40g/1½ oz/⅓ cup dried apricots, soaked and squeezed dry
40g/1½ oz/¼ cup corn kernels
40g/1½ oz goat's cheese, crumbled
4 jumbo quails, fully boned
salt and freshly ground pepper

FOR THE RÖSTI

500g/18oz sweet potatoes, par-boiled with 1 tsp ground cardamom,
  then peeled and grated
½ tsp ground cardamom

FOR THE GARNISH

280g/10oz broccoli florets
125ml/4fl oz/½ cup Cauliflower Cream (see page 184)
12 pieces of sun-dried tomatoes (optional)

To make the stuffing: Sweat the onion in a little oil until soft and translucent, add the garlic and sweat for another minute. Leave to cool.
Pour the milk on to the bread and let it soak in for 10 minutes. Squeeze out all the milk, add the bread to the onions, together with the pork and chicken livers, and mince (grind) through a fine plate or whizz in a food processor until smooth. Add the egg and yolk, and season with salt and pepper. Mix in the apricots, corn and goat's cheese.
To cook the quails: heat the oven to 200°C/400°F/Gas Mark 6. Lay the quails out flat, skin side down, season with salt and pepper,

then fill with about 80g/3oz/½ cup of the stuffing. Shape the quails into their original shape and secure with a toothpick or wooden cocktail stick. Place them on a roasting tray and roast in the oven for 25 minutes. Keep warm.
To make the sweet potato rösti: Place a 10cm/4in round pastry (cookie) cutter in a non-stick frying pan (skillet) or rösti tin (pan), and add a little oil. Season the grated sweet potatoes with salt, pepper and the ground cardamom, put a 1cm/½in layer of sweet potato into the ring, and fry quickly until crispy. Turn the potato over and fry on the other side, then drain on kitchen paper (paper towels). Make 3 more rösti in the same way.
To serve: Place a rösti on each plate, remove the toothpicks or cocktail sticks from the quails and put a bird on top of the rösti. Blanch the broccoli, season it and cover with cauliflower cream. If you wish, garnish the broccoli with the sun-dried tomatoes.

Slow-Braised Young Pork Perfumed with Caraway on Portabello Polenta with Glazed Spring Onions (Scallions)

For this springtime dish, the quality of pork is crucial; it must come from a pig no more than four months old. I use meat from the neck – in my opinion a much under-used cut. But if it is correctly cooked, it is scrumptious, and will give you exactly the amount of fat you will need for this kind of cooking. The caraway adds a lingering and intriguing flavour.

SERVES 4

1.5kg/3¼ lb pork neck, from a young pig
2 tbsp ground caraway seeds
3 tbsp olive oil
400g/14oz mixed vegetables for roasting (onions, garlic, carrots, leeks, celery), cut into 1cm/½ in cubes
3 tbsp tomato purée (paste)
200ml/7fl oz/scant 1 cup dry white wine
400ml/14fl oz/1¾ cups Chicken Stock (see page 180)
1 tsp caraway seeds
2 bunches of spring onions (scallions), trimmed and outside leaves removed, cut into 6cm/2¼in lengths
¼ tsp sugar
salt and freshly ground pepper

FOR THE PORTABELLO MUSHROOM POLENTA

½ garlic bulb
3 tbsp olive oil
150g/5oz portabello mushrooms
500ml/18fl oz/2¼ cups Chicken Stock (see page 180)
120g/4oz/generous ¾ cup polenta
2 tbsp flat parsley leaves
50g/2oz/⅔ cup freshly grated Parmesan cheese

To cook the pork: Heat the oven to 140°C/ 275°F/Gas Mark 1. Season the pork with salt and pepper, and rub in the ground caraway. Heat 2 tbsp olive oil in a flameproof casserole, put in the pork and seal until browned all over. Take out the pork and set it aside.
Add the roasting vegetables to the casserole and fry until browned. Stir in the tomato purée (paste) and stir until slightly caramelized. Add a splash of wine and reduce again until it caramelizes, then repeat another 3 times, until the tomato purée is browned.

Return the pork to the casserole, pour in enough chicken stock to come about one-third of the way up the sides, and add the caraway seeds. Cover and braise slowly in the oven for 4 hours until tender. Stir and turn over the pork frequently, and check that the level of liquid in the casserole remains about the same. If necessary, top it up with more chicken stock.
When the pork is tender, take it out of the cooking liquid, and keep it warm. Increase the oven temperature to 200°C/400°F/Gas Mark 6. Set the casserole on the hob (stovetop) and reduce the cooking liquid by half, then pass it through a fine sieve or muslin (cheesecloth). Season to taste with salt and pepper.
To make the portabello polenta: Break up the bulb of garlic, place on foil and drizzle with 1 tbsp olive oil. Wrap the garlic cloves in the foil. Bake in the hot oven for 45 minutes until soft. Leave to cool, then squeeze out the garlic flesh.
Trim and wipe the mushrooms, and cut into cubes. Heat the remaining olive oil in a frying pan (skillet) and add the mushrooms, season with salt and pepper, and sweat for 2 minutes. Put the stock in a large pan with plenty of salt, bring to the boil, add the mushrooms, then pour in the polenta in a steady stream, stirring as you go. Whisk constantly until it thickens, then turn down the heat as low as possible (or use a heat diffuser), and cook for about 20 minutes, stirring constantly with a wooden spoon. Chop the parsley, add it to the polenta with the Parmesan and roasted garlic pulp, and season with salt and pepper.
To serve: Heat the remaining olive oil in a pan, add the spring onions (scallions) and fry over high heat for 2 minutes. Sprinkle in the sugar and sweat for 2–3 minutes, then add the remaining chicken stock, and simmer until it has evaporated and the onions are soft.
Cut the pork into 1cm/½in thick slices and serve it on a bed of polenta. Top with the spring onions.

Vermicelli-coated Fritto Misto with Couscous and Soft-boiled Egg Sauce

Seafood fritto misto has always been one of my favourite lunch dishes. I came across this unusual idea of wrapping it in vermicelli after eating a langoustine dish in which the crustaceans were enrobed in angel hair pasta. The contrast of the crispy little fried noodles and the softness of the couscous is a perfect mix of textures, and the soft-boiled egg sauce enhances the flavour of the fish.

SERVES 4

2 eggs
40g/1½oz/1½ cups flat parsley, washed and shredded
2 egg yolks
120g/4oz cooked egg vermicelli
150g/5oz halibut, skinned and cut into 2 x 9cm/¾ x 3½in strips
150g/5oz organic salmon, skinned and cut into 2 x 9cm/
    ¾ x 3½in strips
4 langoustines, shelled
4 scallops
40g/1½oz squid, cut into 5mm/¼in rings and quickly blanched
oil, for deep-frying
50g/2oz/2 cups curly parsley leaves, washed and dried
2 lemons, halved and pips removed (optional)
salt and freshly ground pepper

FOR THE COUSCOUS

1 onion, finely chopped
3 tbsp olive oil
50g/2oz/½ cup shelled almonds, coarsely chopped
150ml/5fl oz/⅔ cup dry white wine
250ml/9fl oz/generous 1 cup Chicken Stock (see page 180)
½ cinnamon stick
250g/9oz/1¾ cup couscous
3 tbsp flat parsley, washed and shredded

To make the couscous: In a pan, sweat the onion in the olive oil until soft and translucent, then add the almonds, wine, chicken stock and cinnamon, season and bring to the boil. Add the couscous and stir for 1 minute. When the mixture returns to the boil, reduce the heat to very low, cover the pan, and simmer for 10–15 minutes, until the couscous has absorbed all the liquid. Take the pan off the heat and leave to stand for 5 minutes. Discard the cinnamon, fluff up the couscous grains with a fork, and taste. Adjust the seasoning and stir in the parsley just before serving.
Meanwhile, make the egg sauce: Boil the eggs for 3 minutes, then cut them in half and scoop out the cooked eggs with a spoon (they will still be very runny). Season and stir in the shredded parsley. Keep warm.
Mix the raw egg yolks with the vermicelli. Season all the fish and shellfish, and wrap some vermicelli around them; they do not need to be totally enclosed. Heat the oil to 160°C/320°F. Quickly drop in the curly parsley and fry until crispy. Drain on kitchen paper (paper towels).
Using the same oil, fry the vermicelli-wrapped fish and shellfish in separate batches until just golden brown; take care not to overcook them. Drain on kitchen paper.
To serve: Place the fried fish on a plate with the deep-fried parsley and lemon, if using. Serve the egg sauce in a small dipping bowl and the couscous on the side.

Famous Faces at The Savoy

From princes to pop stars, the hotel has been a mecca for celebrities since the day it opened in August 1898. Writers, artists, musicians, ballet dancers, stars of stage and screen all have drawn inspiration from the refined atmosphere and chic surroundings of The Savoy.

From the outset, the inimitable duo of manager César Ritz and chef de cuisine Auguste Escoffier acted as a magnet for the high society of the day. Their drawing power made it acceptable for women to dine out, and fashionable society leaders such as Mrs Keppel and Lady de Grey began to host elegant fun-filled dinner parties at The Savoy. The ultimate recommendation came when the Prince of Wales (later Edward V11) dined with Lily Langtry. The Savoy became the "in" place to dine and stay, and since that visit, royalty of every kind – British, European and "American" – has regularly patronized the hotel.

Situated so close to theatreland, The Savoy became a popular after-show meeting place for a host of theatrical and musical stars. Dame Nellie Melba (almost as famous for the eponymous peach dessert as for her operatic skills) lived in the hotel for a year, to the disgust of her great rival Adelina Patti. The two divas detested one another, and had to be seated as far apart as possible when dining in the same restaurant. All the flamboyant and histrionic thespians of their day – Sarah Bernhardt, Noel Coward and Gertrude Lawrence, Ivor Novello, Charlie Chaplin and even the reclusive Greta Garbo have stayed or dined at The Savoy, and it still attracts the film stars of today.

Of the many artists who stayed at The Savoy, inspired by its superb situation overlooking the Thames, the most famous was Monet, who painted the river views, including Waterloo and Charing Cross bridges and the Houses of Parliament, that he saw from his rooms on the fifth and sixth floors. James McNeill Whistler made a sketch of the scaffolding during the building of the hotel in the 1880s, remarking that it would "never look so well again". He changed his view, however, when he later returned to paint the Thames from his balcony. In 1910, two more storeys were added, and Oscar Kokoschka was able to paint the broadest river vista of all from his eyrie on the eighth floor.

The Savoy has welcomed its share of famous writers, too. The most infamous was Oscar Wilde, a frequent visitor who, at the time of his bankruptcy and imprisonment, owed the hotel £86 – the price of at least a fortnight's stay. In 1930, the novelist Arnold Bennett immortalized the hotel, its backstage workings and the staff in his novel *Imperial Palace* (and was rewarded with a glorious omelette in his name). 2002 saw the start of a new literary tradition, when Fay Weldon became The Savoy's first writer-in-residence. Her three-month tenure included duties as diverse as hosting heavyweight Arts and Science dinners to judging the staff Halloween pumpkin-carving competition. The Savoy hopes to appoint more writers-in-residence to continue its rich theatrical, artistic and literary tradition.

Savoy Summer Pudding

I often wonder who created the summer pudding, an all-time classic that makes the most of the best the season can offer. It's a unique way to use bread, too, as a really tasty filler. This pudding looks as good as it tastes, and is the perfect way to round off a lazy summer lunch.

MAKES 4 INDIVIDUAL PUDDINGS

8 thin slices of day-old white bread, crusts removed
150g/5oz/1 cup strawberries, hulled
150g/5oz/1¼ cups blueberries
50g/2oz/⅓ cup raspberries
50g/2oz/½ cup redcurrants, stripped off the stalks
50g/2oz/¼ cup caster (superfine) sugar

FOR THE DECORATION

Raspberry Sauce (see page 184)
50ml/2fl oz/¼ cup double (heavy) cream, stiffly whipped
4 mint sprigs
4 clusters of redcurrants
4 strawberries, hulled
a few hulled raspberries and blackberries
a few blueberries
icing (confectioners') sugar, to serve

Cut out 4 rounds of bread slightly smaller than the top of a dariole mould. Cut the remaining bread into 1cm/½in strips, and use these to line the base and sides of 4 dariole moulds.
Put all the fruit in a pan with the caster (superfine) sugar, and simmer over a moderate heat, stirring occasionally, for about 5 minutes until the fruit is tender and the syrup is slightly reduced. Fill the bread-lined moulds with the hot fruit and syrup. Allow the bread to soak up the syrup, then add extra fruit as necessary to fill each mould completely. Top each with a round of bread. Cover and chill overnight.
Unmould the summer puddings on to individual plates. Spoon some raspberry sauce over each pudding, pipe on a rosette of cream and top with a mint sprig. Dust the redcurrant clusters and uncooked berries with icing (confectioners') sugar, and use them to decorate the plates.

Riesling-marinated Berries with Elderflower Sorbet (Sherbet)

This is a very light and delightful dessert, which is quickly made and perfect for a summer lunch. Elderflower sorbet (sherbet) is the perfect accompaniment in season, but you can use any other sorbet or ice cream if you prefer.

SERVES 4

FOR THE LIME MARINADE

juice of 3 limes
150ml/5fl oz/⅔ cup Riesling wine
4 tbsp crème de cassis (blackcurrant liqueur)
50g/2oz/½ cup icing (confectioners') sugar
2 tsp chopped mint leaves
350g/12oz/3 cups mixed summer berries (eg: raspberries, strawberries, blackberries, blueberries and loganberries)
4 mint sprigs, to garnish

FOR THE ELDERFLOWER SORBET (SHERBET)

150g/5oz/¾ cup caster (superfine) sugar
350ml/12fl oz/1½ cups water
350ml/12fl oz/1½ cups elderflower syrup

To make the elderflower sorbet (sherbet): Put the sugar and water in a pan and dissolve over a low heat, then bring to the boil. Remove from the heat and add the elderflower syrup. Leave to cool completely, then churn in an ice cream maker. Alternatively, pour the mixture into a large freezerproof bowl, cover and freeze until almost set.
Transfer to a food processor and whizz to break down the ice crystals. Return the mixture to the bowl, cover and freeze again for 3 hours until almost set. Repeat the process once more to obtain a fine-textured sorbet. Cover and freeze for another 2 hours. Just before serving, mash the sorbet well with a fork.
To make the lime marinade: Mix together the lime juice, Riesling and crème de cassis. Stir in the sugar and whisk to mix thoroughly. Stir in the chopped mint, cover and chill for at least 1 hour. Pass through a fine sieve.
Rinse the berries and dry them carefully. Divide them among 4 deep serving dishes, such as small soup plates. Spoon the lime marinade over the berries.
To serve: Shape the sorbet into quenelles by dipping a dessert spoon in hot water and scraping it across the surface of the sorbet, rolling it into the spoon to make a neat shape. Place a quenelle of sorbet on top of the berries, garnish with a sprig of mint, and serve.

Passion Fruit Tart

I have always been keen on tarts and without doubt this modest passion fruit tart is one of the simplest and best. Like its better known and often-copied cousin, lemon tart, its sharpness is the key to its success. I think this version is superior because of the natural intensity of the passion fruit, and the seeds add a welcome coarse texture.

The pastry base is unusual, as it is baked slowly at low temperature, giving the gluten time to develop and create a very firm (not doughy), liquid-resistant pastry, which is ideal for this kind of tart. The addition of almonds adds a more intense flavour and texture.

SERVES 8

FOR THE PASTRY

250g/9oz/2¼ cups plain (all-purpose) flour
generous pinch of salt
120g/4oz/½ cup unsalted (sweet) butter, at room temperature
80g/3oz/¾ cup icing (confectioners') sugar, sifted
1 egg, lightly beaten
50g/2oz/½ cup ground almonds

FOR THE FILLING AND SAUCE

500ml/18fl oz/2¼ cups passion fruit juice
400g/14oz/2 cups sugar
9 eggs
250ml/9fl oz/generous 1 cup whipping cream
6 whole passion fruit, halved and seeds and juice scraped out
½ tsp cornflour (cornstarch)

To make the pastry: Sift the flour and salt together. Cream the butter until pale and fluffy. With a wooden spoon, mix in the sifted icing (confectioners') sugar, then the beaten egg, and stir until the mixture is smooth. Add the sifted flour, ground almonds and salt, and knead lightly with your fingertips to make a dough. Shape it into a ball, wrap in cling film (plastic wrap), and chill in the refrigerator overnight.

To bake the pastry case (pie shell): Heat the oven to 160°C/325°F/Gas Mark 3. Roll out the dough as thinly as possible (3mm/⅛in thick), and line a flan ring (quiche pan) with it. Do not prick the base, or the filling will run out when you bake the tart. Cover the base with greaseproof (waxed) paper or cling film, and fill to the top with baking beans.
Bake blind (without filling) in the oven for about 40 minutes. Remove the baking beans and greaseproof paper or cling film, and bake for a further 5 minutes until the pastry is evenly coloured.

To make the filling: Boil the passion fruit juice to reduce it by half, and leave to cool. Mix together 350g/12oz/1¾ cups sugar and the eggs, then mix in the cream and reduced passion fruit juice. Pass the mixture through a fine sieve, then add the seeds of 3 of the passion fruit, and whisk until thoroughly mixed.

To cook the tart: Heat the oven to 150°C/300°F/Gas Mark 2. Pour the filling into the pastry case and bake the tart in the oven for 30 minutes, or until the filling has set. Cool to room temperature and cut into 8 slices.

To make the sauce: Mix a small quantity of the remaining passion fruit seeds and sugar with the cornflour (cornstarch). Put the rest in a small pan and heat gently until boiling, then whisk in the cornflour mixture.

To serve: Place a slice of passion fruit tart on each plate and pour a little of the sauce around it.

Gratinated Pink Grapefruit
with Basil Ice Cream

This most refreshing lunchtime dessert can be whipped up very quickly, and looks and tastes delicious. You can substitute any other fruit for the grapefruit, or even use a mixture of fruits, choosing whatever is in season.

SERVES 4

FOR THE SABAYON

5 egg yolks
80g/3oz/scant ½ cup caster (superfine) sugar
100ml/3½fl oz/scant ½ cup grappa
juice of ½ an orange
juice of 1 lemon
125ml/4fl oz/½ cup double (heavy) cream, lightly whipped
4 pink grapefruit, segmented (all seeds, pith and membrane removed)
160g/5½ oz Basil Ice Cream (see page 188)
3 tsp pink praline (see recipe right)

FOR THE TUILE BASKETS

100g/3½oz/scant 1 cup plain (all-purpose) flour
100g/3½oz/scant 1 cup icing (confectioners') sugar
100g/3½oz/scant ½ cup unsalted (sweet) butter, melted
2 egg whites

To make the sabayon: Bring a pan of water to just below boiling point to make a bain-marie. Put the egg yolks, caster (superfine) sugar, grappa, orange and lemon juice in a wide bowl, set it over the simmering water, making sure that the base of the bowl is not in direct contact with the water, and whisk until the mixture doubles in volume. Transfer it to an electric mixer, and whisk until cold. Fold in the lightly whipped cream, and place in the refrigerator.
To make the baskets: Heat the oven to 220°C/425°F/Gas Mark 7. Sift the flour and icing (confectioners') sugar into a mixing bowl. Quickly stir in the melted butter and egg whites to make a smooth paste. Chill for 30 minutes. Spread the chilled mixture very thinly on a greased baking tray (cookie sheet). Bake in the oven for 8–10 minutes. While still warm, cut into 4 rounds with a 8cm/3¼in pastry (cookie) cutter, then place in cups to shape into baskets. Heat the grill (broiler) to very hot. Spread a 1cm/½ in layer of sabayon on four heatproof plates, arrange the grapefruit segments on top, and quickly glaze under the very hot grill.
Place a basket in the middle and arrange a ball of basil ice cream in it. Sprinkle with the pink praline.

PINK PRALINE

MAKES 250G/9OZ/2¼ CUPS

3 tbsp water
100g/3½oz/scant ½ cup sugar
1 tsp liquid glucose
100g/3½oz white chocolate
a drop of red food colouring
40 pistachio nuts

Put the water, sugar and glucose in a pan and boil until it becomes an amber-coloured syrup. Leave to cool.
Melt the white chocolate in a bain-marie or microwave. Stir the melted chocolate, food colouring and pistachios into the cooled syrup. Pour on to a sheet of greaseproof (waxed) paper and leave to cool, then chop the praline into very small pieces. It will keep for up to 1 week in an airtight container

Sticky Toffee and Apple Pudding with Crème Fraîche

Normally we think of sticky toffee pudding as a heavy and wintry lunchtime pudding. This is the exception; it is as light as anything you can think of and I think it's worth all the calories and more.

SERVES 4

2 Granny Smith apples
juice of ½ lemon
100ml/3½fl oz/scant ½ cup Stock Syrup (see page 185)
100g/3½ oz/¾ cup sultanas (golden raisins)
80g/3oz/⅔ cup dates, stoned (pitted)
1 tsp bicarbonate of soda (baking soda)
25g/1oz/2 tbsp unsalted (sweet) butter
75g/2½ oz/⅓ cup sugar
2 eggs
2 tsp baking powder
75g/2½oz/generous ½ cup plain (all-purpose) flour

FOR THE TOFFEE SAUCE

100g/3½oz/scant ½ cup demerara (raw) sugar
50g/2oz/¼ cup butter
3 tbsp double (heavy) cream
3 tbsp Calvados
100ml/3½fl oz/scant ½ cup crème fraîche, to serve

FOR THE APPLE AND SULTANA (GOLDEN RAISIN) SAUCE

2 tsp pectin
500ml/18fl oz/2 cups freshly pressed apple juice
80g/3oz/scant cup caster (superfine) sugar

Peel one of the apples and scoop out small balls with a parisienne (melon) baller. Keep them in the lemon juice to avoid discoloration. Core the remaining apple and cut it into very thin rings with a mandoline or food processor. Lay them on a sheet of silicone paper and brush with stock syrup. Leave to dry out in a warm place (such as an airing cupboard or a very low oven) at about 80°C/180°F or the lowest gas setting for about 4 hours.

Simmer the sultanas (golden raisins) in 5 tbsp water for 10 minutes, leave them to plump up for about 1 hour, then lift them out of the water and cut them in half.

Simmer the dates and bicarbonate of soda (baking soda) in the same water for 10 minutes, and leave to cool.

Heat the oven to 200°C/400°F/Gas Mark 6. Cream the butter and sugar together. Whisk the eggs and slowly stir them into the sugar and butter mix. Add the baking powder, then the date mixture. Pour into a lined and buttered 20cm/8in deep ovenproof dish and bake in the oven for 35 minutes.

To make the toffee sauce: Combine the sugar, butter and cream in a pan. Bring to the boil and stir in the Calvados. Keep warm.

After 35 minutes, take the sticky toffee pudding out of the oven and pour some of the toffee sauce over it. Return it to the oven for another 10 minutes, then cut it into triangles.

To make the apple and sultana sauce: Mix the pectin with the apple juice and sugar and boil for 5 minutes. Cool, then add the apple balls, lemon juice and sultanas. If the mixture is too thick, just return it to the heat for a moment.

To serve: Place a warm triangle of sticky toffee pudding on each plate, and pour the apple and sultana sauce around it. Put a spoonful of crème fraîche on top and garnish with an apple ring.

Mango and Mascarpone Ice Cream
with Home-made Biscotti

This is very simple, quite delicious recipe always pleases our guests, and they usually ask for more! It makes the perfect finish to a lunch, and also looks pleasingly healthy. Sadly, it is not quite so healthy as it seems – but what good food is?

SERVES 4

500ml/18fl oz/2¼ cups mango purée
6 egg yolks
200g/7oz/scant 1 cup sugar
zest of ½ lemon
250g/9oz/generous 1 cup mascarpone cheese
250ml/9fl oz/generous 1 cup crème fraîche
2 tbsp Grand Marnier
½ vanilla pod (bean)

FOR THE GARNISH

1 medium-sized ripe mango
200ml/7fl oz/scant 1 cup Stock Syrup (see page 185)
8 biscotti (see recipe right)
4 small mint sprigs

Boil the mango purée until reduced to 350ml/12fl oz/1½ cups. Whisk the egg yolks and sugar until creamy, then pour on the hot mango purée, stirring constantly. Add the lemon zest.
Return the mixture to the pan and bring back to the boil, stirring with a wooden spoon, until the mixture has thickened slightly and coats the back of the spoon.
Take off the heat and whisk in the mascarpone, crème fraîche and half the Grand Marnier, then pass through a fine sieve. Scrape in the seeds from the vanilla pod (bean), and whisk. Leave to cool, then churn in an ice cream maker until frozen. Alternatively, pour the mixture into a large freezerproof bowl, cover and freeze until almost set. Transfer to a food processor and whizz to break down the ice crystals. Return the mixture to the bowl, cover and freeze again for 3 hours until almost set. Repeat the process once more to obtain a very smooth ice cream.
To make the garnish: Peel and halve the mango, remove the stone (pit), and cut the flesh into very fine slices.

Heat the stock syrup, add the remaining Grand Marnier, pour over the sliced mango and leave to infuse (steep) for 5 minutes.
To serve: If the ice cream has been stored in the freezer for a while and has gone hard, transfer it to the refrigerator for 20–30 minutes before serving to soften slightly.
Arrange the mango slices on 4 plates and top with a ball of mango ice cream. Garnish with biscotti and a mint sprig.

BISCOTTI

MAKES 20–24 BISCOTTI

1 star anise
220g/8oz/2 cups plain (all-purpose) flour
130g/4½oz/generous 1 cup icing (confectioners') sugar
pinch of salt
3 eggs, lightly beaten
finely grated zest of 1 orange
100g/3½ oz/scant 1 cup blanched almonds
  (or any nut you choose), toasted

Using a pestle and mortar, grind the star anise to a fine powder. Sift the flour, sugar and salt into a bowl, and make a well in the centre. Put the eggs, ground star anise and grated orange zest in the well and mix thoroughly to a sticky dough. Knead in the almonds.
Shape the dough into a log, about 4cm/1½in diameter. Wrap in non-stick baking parchment and chill in the freezer for 1 hour until firm.
Heat the oven to 180°C/350°F/Gas Mark 4. Place the dough log, still wrapped in the baking parchment, on a baking sheet (cookie sheet), and bake in the oven for 50–55 minutes.
Leave to cool, then cut the log into 20–24 very thin slices, about 2mm/⅒ in thick. Carefully transfer to a wire rack and leave to dry.

Chocolate and Coffee Fantasia

I should love to claim this fantastic dessert as my own but I have to admit that it was created by a Savoy pastry chef, Rob. Although it looks complicated, it is actually quite simple to make; all you need is a little forward planning so that you don't leave everything to the last moment. The chocolate tuiles can be made the day before and kept in airtight containers.

SERVES 4

FOR THE MOUSSE

150g/5oz best quality plain (semi-sweet) chocolate
25g/1oz/2 tbsp caster (superfine) sugar
2 egg yolks
175ml/6fl oz/¾ cup whipping cream

FOR THE COFFEE GRANITA

80g/3oz/scant ½ cup sugar
500ml/18fl oz/2¼ cups double strength coffee

FOR THE CHOCOLATE TUILES

25g/1oz/¼ cup (unsweetened) cocoa powder
120g/4oz/1 cup icing (confectioners') sugar
100g/3½oz/generous ¾ cup plain (all-purpose) flour
4 egg whites
150g/5oz/⅔ cup unsalted (sweet) butter, melted

To make the chocolate mousse: Break up the chocolate in a large heatproof bowl and set it over a pan of simmering water until melted. Put the sugar in a pan with 1 tbsp water, and heat to 121°C/250°F. If you don't have a sugar thermometer, boil until you have a clear syrup.
Put the egg yolks in an electric mixer and whisk, then gradually pour on the syrup and continue whisking until the yolks have at least doubled in volume. Keep whisking until cooled. In a separate bowl, whip the cream to the ribbon stage, and fold it into the egg yolk mixture. Stir one-third into the melted chocolate, then fold in the rest. Chill in the refrigerator.

To make the granita: Stir the sugar into the coffee until dissolved. Pour it into a shallow tray and place in the freezer until half-frozen. Stir the mixture with a fork to break up the ice crystals. Return it to the freezer until half frozen again, and repeat this operation 4–5 times until the granita forms small, firm iced flakes.
To make the chocolate tuiles: Heat the oven to 200°C/400°F/Gas Mark 6. Sift together the cocoa, icing (confectioners') sugar and flour, then stir in the egg whites, followed by the melted butter. Place in the refrigerator for at least 1 hour.
Using a sheet of plastic, cut out four 7cm/2¾in round stencils and eight triangles, 4.5cm/1¾in at the base and 12cm/4¾in high. Cut two holes in each triangle for decoration. Place the stencils on a silicone mat on a baking tray (cookie sheet) and spread the tuile mixture over them Bake for 8–10 minutes, until golden brown. Mould the round tuiles inside a small bowl, or cup, 1 at a time, so that they take on the shape of the bowl.
To serve: Place a tuile bowl on each plate, fill with the granita, and top with a small ball of chocolate mousse. Lay a wavy tuile over it. Pour a little chocolate sauce around.

Afternoon Tea

There is no more delightful and quintessentially British institution than afternoon tea – and nowhere better to enjoy it than in the elegant Thames Foyer at The Savoy. Waiters calmly move through the Foyer dressed in their elegant black waistcoats (vests) and jackets; the ritual of tea is strictly observed as guests are served from white china pots; three-tiered cake stands overflow with dainty sandwiches; and freshly-baked scones and pretty pastries are served in crinkly paper cases. In the background, a pianist plays on The Savoy's white grand piano, while a mix of residents and guests – from county ladies in smart dresses and even occasionally hats, to American tourists in trainers and practical rainwear – enjoy a traditional English tea.

Times change, however, and tradition must be updated. At The Savoy, we offer a choice of teas including our own exclusive blends from China and Sri Lanka. Fragrant, astringent, smoky or flowery – all our teas are served in specially designed teapots, and our sandwiches are given a modern twist with home-baked herb and tomato flavoured breads. Fillings for featherlight fruit tartlets vary with the seasons, and at Easter we offer a chocolate afternoon tea with a glass of champagne. What could be more civilized?

"Thank God for tea", wrote the Reverend Sidney Smith. "What would the world do without tea? I am glad I was not born before tea." Whether you come to nibble on a delicate crustless cucumber sandwich, spoon clotted cream and jam on to a saffron and raisin scone, sink your teeth into a cream-filled choux pastry swan, or simply to people watch – to see and be seen – afternoon tea at The Savoy is an indulgence not to be missed.

Savoy Sandwiches

At The Savoy, the chefs pride themselves on offering an interesting selection of sandwiches made with a variety of breads, including their own tomato and basil breads for added flavour. Unlike other hotels, where the teatime sandwiches are usually cut into dainty squares, The Savoy's are always cut into fingers (bars), which I find more elegant.

CREAM CHEESE AND MARMITE SANDWICHES

MAKES 6 SANDWICHES

4 slices of white bread
2–3 tsp Marmite
40g/1½oz/3 tbsp cream cheese (such as Philadelphia)

Spread 2 slices of bread very thinly with Marmite. Spread the cream cheese on the other two slices and put together with Marmite slices to make sandwiches.
Cut off the crusts and cut each sandwich into 3 equal fingers (bars).

CUCUMBER SANDWICHES WITH EGG AND MINT

MAKES 6 SANDWICHES

2 hard-boiled (hard-cooked) eggs, peeled and finely grated
2 tbsp crème fraîche
½ bunch of mint, leaves picked off and finely chopped
4 slices of white bread, buttered
½ cucumber, peeled and thinly sliced
salt and freshly ground pepper

Mix the eggs with the crème fraîche and mint, and season with salt and pepper. Spread the mixture 5mm/¼in thick on 2 slices of bread. Top with the sliced cucumber, and make into sandwiches with the remaining bread. Cut off the crusts and cut each sandwich into 3 equal fingers (bars).

CREAMED AVOCADO, PLUM TOMATO AND RED ONION SANDWICHES ON BASIL BREAD

MAKES 6 SANDWICHES

1 avocado, peeled and stoned (pitted)
4 tbsp crème fraîche
1 plum tomato, peeled, de-seeded and finely diced
½ small red onion, finely chopped
4 slices of basil bread, buttered
salt and freshly ground pepper

Mash the avocado with the crème fraîche. Stir in the diced tomato and chopped red onion and season to taste. Fill the bread with this mixture to make 2 sandwiches. Cut off the crusts and cut each sandwich into 3 equal fingers (bars).

PRAWN (SHRIMP) AND SPRING ONION (SCALLION) SANDWICHES WITH SUN-DRIED TOMATO BREAD

MAKES 6 SANDWICHES

100g/3½oz/scant 1 cup cooked, peeled prawns (shrimp)
2 spring onions (scallions), finely chopped
2 tbsp mayonnaise-based cocktail sauce
4 slices of sun-dried tomato bread, buttered
salt and freshly ground pepper

Mix together the prawns (shrimp), spring onions (scallions) and cocktail sauce, and season with salt and pepper. Make into 2 sandwiches with the bread. Cut off the crusts and cut each sandwich into 3 equal fingers (bars).

H·M·S PINAFORE

-or The Lass that loved a Sailor.

The Savoy Theatre

The Savoy Theatre stands adjacent to The Savoy Hotel, attached to it by a vast steel beam. The connection between a hotel and a theatre may seem tenuous, but the link is Richard d'Oyly Carte, the Irish musical impresario who was the genius behind the two organizations.

In 1875, d'Oyly Carte started a light opera company based at London's Royalty Theatre. He planned to open the season with an Offenbach operetta, but it proved too short to fill an entire evening. Not wishing to short-change his audience, d'Oyly Carte needed to find a filler fast.

By chance, he encountered the librettist W.S. Gilbert, who offered a comic skit set in a law court to fill the gap. D'Oyly Carte at once commissioned Arthur Sullivan to write the music. A flurry of rehearsals followed – and *Trial by Jury* was conceived and born in a matter of weeks. It was an instant success; the trio of impresario, librettist and composer was immediately accorded the status of greatest collaboration in British theatrical history.

Unheard-of wealth and fame quickly followed. The d'Oyly Carte Company moved to the Opéra Comique Theatre and the whole of London flocked to see their operettas. Within five years, the theatre had become far too small to accommodate the crowds of Gilbert and Sullivan fans, all desperate to see the latest G and S shows. D'Oyly Carte decided to invest his share of the annual £60,000 profits in building a new theatre for the company. His chosen site was a parcel of disused land where once the Savoy Palace had stood in the Middle Ages.

The state-of-the-art theatre boasted every desirable design feature of the time and was the first public building in the world to replace old-fashioned gas lamps with electric lights. The public loved it and flocked to see its contemporary design; the stampede for tickets caused Richard d'Oyly Carte to invent the concept of a queue to control the crowds, serving the public with tea and cakes while they waited to buy tickets for the show.

Saffron Scones with Raisins

Saffron brings richness and flavour to these teatime favourites. Given the Savoy treatment, topped with clotted cream and soft fruit, they are a real luxury.

MAKES 8

generous pinch of saffron threads
150ml/5fl oz/²⁄₃ cup white wine
250g/9oz/2¼ cups strong plain (all-purpose) flour,
   plus extra for dusting
1 tbsp baking powder
50g/2oz/¼ cup caster (superfine) sugar
80g/3oz/6 tbsp unsalted (sweet) butter, cubed,
   plus extra for greasing
100–125ml/3½–4fl oz/about ½ cup milk
50g/2oz/⅓ cup raisins
1 egg, beaten

FOR SERVING

butter or clotted cream
fresh fruit (optional)
10 tiny mint sprigs (optional)

Heat the oven to 220°C/425°F/Gas Mark 7. Put the saffron and wine in a small pan and boil until reduced to 1 tbsp. Pass through a fine sieve and reserve the liquid.

Sift the flour and baking powder together, then stir in the sugar. Rub in the butter until the mixture resembles breadcrumbs. Add the saffron liquid and sufficient milk to form a soft, smooth dough, then work in the raisins. On a lightly floured surface, roll out the dough to 2cm/¾in thick, and stamp out 10 rounds with a 6cm/2¾in pastry (cookie) cutter. (Do not overwork the dough as it may go hard.) Place the scones on a greased baking (cookie) sheet, brush the tops with beaten egg. Leave to rest for 15 minutes in a cool place, brush again with egg and bake for about 15 minutes until risen and golden brown.

Cut the scones in half and serve with butter or clotted cream. Alternatively, spread on a little clotted cream, top with fresh fruit in season, and garnish with a tiny sprig of mint.

Herb Scones with White Crab Meat and Salmon Caviar

These savoury scones are a delicious and sophisticated alternative to sandwiches – or, of course, if you hungry, you will tuck into both!

MAKES 6

250g/9oz/2¼ cups strong white bread flour,
   plus extra for dusting
1 tbsp baking powder
80g/3oz/6 tbsp unsalted (sweet) butter, cubed,
   plus extra for greasing
4 tsp chopped mixed herbs (eg: basil, rosemary,
   marjoram and oregano)
125ml/4fl oz/½ cup milk
1 egg, lightly beaten

FOR THE TOPPING

100ml/3½fl oz/scant ½ cup crème fraîche
150g/5oz white crab meat
50g/2oz cucumber, peeled, de-seeded and diced
salt and freshly ground pepper

FOR THE GARNISH

mixed lettuce leaves
1 tbsp salmon caviar (keta)
dill sprigs

Heat the oven to 220°C/425°F/Gas Mark 7. Sift the flour and baking powder into a bowl, then rub in the butter until the mixture resembles breadcrumbs. Stir in the herbs. Add the milk and work to a soft dough.

On a lightly floured surface, roll out the dough to 2cm/¾in thick. Stamp out six 6cm/2¾in rounds with a pastry (cookie) cutter. (Do not overwork the dough as it may go hard.) Place the scones on a greased baking (cookie) sheet and brush the tops with beaten egg. Bake for about 15 minutes until risen and golden brown. Leave to cool.

Mix the crème fraîche with the crab meat and cucumber, and season with salt and pepper. Arrange a few small lettuce leaves on the edge of each scone. Heap a generous amount of crab meat on each, add a teaspoon spoonful of salmon caviar and garnish the top with sprigs of dill.

Savoy Choux Pastry Swans

At George Kessler's famous gondola party in 1905 (you can read about it on page 99), a gâteau was served with these delicate swans on top. I liked the idea of the swans and The Savoy now serves them alone for afternoon tea.

MAKES 10

150g/5oz Choux Paste (see page 187)
butter, for greasing
25g/1oz/2 tbsp caster (superfine) sugar
750ml/1¼ pints/3 cups double (heavy) cream
icing (confectioners') sugar for dusting

Heat the oven to 200°C/400°F/Gas Mark 6. Put the choux paste in a piping (pastry) bag fitted with a 1cm/½in nozzle (tip), and pipe ten 2.5cm/1in rounds on to a buttered baking tray (cookie sheet). Bake the choux buns for 15 minutes, then leave to cool.
Reduce the oven temperature to 180°C/350°F/Gas Mark 4. Using a 3mm/⅛in plain nozzle, pipe ten "S" shapes of choux paste on to another buttered baking tray. Bake for 10 minutes or until golden brown and crispy, then leave to cool.
Add the caster sugar to the cream and whip until just firm. Put the whipped cream into a piping bag with a small star nozzle.
Cut off the top third of the buns. Pipe the cream into the base of the choux buns to fill. Cut the top third of the buns in half and place both pieces in the cream at an angle, to give the impression of a pair of wings. Place the "S"-shaped pastry at the front of each bun to make the swan's neck. Dust each swan with icing (confectioners') sugar.

Cinnamon Madeleines

There are numerous stories about who first thought up these small shell-shaped cakes. One theory is that they were created in the seventeenth century by Madeleine Simonin, the personal cook of the Cardinal de Retz in north-eastern France. Apparently, the Cardinal was so delighted with the little cakes that he christened them Madeleines in her honour.

MAKES 15

3 eggs
175g/6oz/scant 1 cup caster (superfine) sugar
250g/9oz/2¼ cups plain (all-purpose) flour
1½ tsp baking powder
1¼ tsp ground cinnamon
5 tbsp milk
120g/4oz/½ cup unsalted (sweet) butter, heated
  to blood temperature
butter and flour for greasing

Beat together the eggs and sugar until creamy. Sift the flour, baking powder and cinnamon into a bowl, add the egg mixture, then the milk gradually. Mix until smooth. Add the melted butter and beat until completely combined. Place the mixture in the refrigerator and leave to rest for 20 minutes.
Heat the oven to 190°C/375°F/Gas Mark 5. Pipe the mixture into greased and floured shell-shaped madeleine moulds (if you don't have these, use 5cm/2in paper cases). Bake the madeleines for 6 minutes. Remove from the moulds and cool on a wire rack.

Exotic Fruit Tartlets

When making teatime Strawberry tartlets (opposite), I decided to use filo pastry instead of the more traditional sweet shortcrust, just to change the texture and balance the whole experience of afternoon tea. Here, I use puff pastry instead of sweet pastry, and add passion fruit to give a nice sharp contrast. The tartlets can be prepared in advance, then filled with the cream and fruit a few hours in advance.

MAKES 4

flour, for dusting
120g/4oz Puff Pastry (see page 186)
½ quantity Frangipane (see page 187)
1 tbsp passion fruit juice, sieved
4 tbsp Pastry Cream (see page 185) or whipped cream
½ kiwi fruit, peeled and sliced
¼ mango, peeled, stoned (pitted) and sliced
¼ small pineapple, peeled, cored and sliced
¼ papaya, peeled, cored and sliced
4 tbsp apricot jam (jelly), warmed and sieved, for glazing
4 tiny mint sprigs

Heat the oven to 200°C/400°F/Gas Mark 6. On a lightly floured surface, roll out the puff pastry thinly and use it to line four 7.5cm/3 in tartlet tins (muffin pans). Leave to rest in a cool place for 15 minutes.
Divide the frangipane among the pastry cases (shells) and bake in the oven for 10–15 minutes until golden brown. Leave to cool.
Stir the passion fruit juice into the pastry cream or whipped cream and spoon it into the tartlets. Arrange the fruit decoratively on top, brush with the apricot jam (jelly), and decorate with the mint.

Strawberry Tartlets

Normally, fruit tartlets are made with sweet shortcrust. Most hotel afternoon tea menus include two or three different tartlets, all made in the same sweet pastry cases. This can be quite heavy and filling, so some years ago the chefs decided to lighten things up a little and make a change. These strawberry tartlets are made with filo pastry. Their very different texture and taste makes an excellent contrast to all the other tartlets. Traditionalists can just replace the filo with sweet shortcrust.

MAKES 4

3 sheets of filo pasty
4 tsp unsalted (sweet) butter, melted
40g/2oz/½ cup icing (confectioners') sugar
½ quantity Frangipane (see page 187)
2 tsp crème de framboise liqueur (optional)
4 tbsp Pastry Cream (see page 185) or whipped cream
14 medium strawberries, hulled
4 tbsp strawberry jam (jelly), warmed and sieved, for glazing
a few skinned and chopped pistachio nuts, to decorate

Heat the oven to 200°C/400°F/Gas Mark 6. Brush 1 sheet of filo pastry with the melted butter and dust with sugar. Lay another sheet on top and brush and dust with more butter and sugar, then add the final sheet and brush and dust again. Cut out four 10cm/4in rounds and use them to line four 7.5cm/2¾ in tartlet tins (muffin pans). Divide the frangipane among the pastry cases (shells) and bake for about 20 minutes until golden. Leave to cool.
If you are using it, stir the framboise liqueur into the pastry cream or whipped cream and pile it into the centre of each tartlet, keeping it away from the edges, or it will flow out when the fruit is pressed on. Cut the strawberries into 4 and arrange on top of the cream. Brush with strawberry jam (jelly) to glaze and sprinkle a few chopped pistachios on top.

Dinner

Dinner at The Savoy is always an elegant affair. In all the restaurants, the waiters exchange their short black dinner jackets (tuxedos) for stylish evening tail coats. The lights are dimmed to create a different ambience, and the menus offer sophisticated dishes to be enjoyed at leisure. Dinner is a romantic occasion, enhanced by the lights reflected in the river outside and the tinkling of the grand piano inside. No one is in a hurry. People come to soak up the atmosphere and take their time choosing from the special three-course dinner menu or the à la carte. No need to hurry back to work, so there is time to peruse the magnificent wine list and indulge in happy anticipation of the gastronomic delights to come.

This is when the brigade of eighty chefs can show off their skills to their best advantage, using luxurious, extravagant ingredients – sautéed goose liver and langoustines, lobster Thermidor, delicious creations of fish and shellfish, the finest Welsh lamb, Scottish beef and game in season. The Savoy's motto is "For Excellence We Strive" – and the staff aim to reach the pinnacle of excellence at dinner.

Meanwhile, in the private banqueting suites, the chefs and waiters may be catering for a lavish evening party – for 500 guests in the Lancaster Room, perhaps, or an extra-special intimate "dîner à deux". Perhaps there is a meeting of a dining club, like The Other Club, founded by Winston Churchill in 1911, whose thirty or so members (politicians and lawyers) still hold their monthly dinners at The Savoy. And as the battalions of diners leave at the end of a memorable evening, another army moves in – the all-important cleaners and dishwashers, whose task is to restore The Savoy restaurants to their pre-dinner glory.

Tomato Consommé with Truffled Mascarpone Tortellini

When I was an apprentice in Ulm in Germany, the head chef used to say that a good kitchen can always be recognized by the quality of its consommé. Sadly, this type of soup seems to have gone out of fashion nowadays, yet every time I have it I wonder why. A good consommé has a rich, intense flavour, which will warm you and restore your energy in winter, or, when eaten chilled in the summer will refresh and cool you. The quantities given may seem daunting, but it is really not possible to make a smaller amount successfully, and you will be well rewarded for your efforts.

SERVES 8–10

FOR THE CONSOMMÉ

100g/3½oz beef shin meat, minced (ground)
100g/3½oz chicken leg meat, chopped
80g/3oz (total weight) carrots, celery, leek and onions, chopped
100g/3½oz/⅓ cup tomato purée (paste)
100g/4oz fresh plum tomatoes, chopped
1 thyme sprig
1 bay leaf
1 tsp crushed black peppercorns

8 egg whites
600ml/1pint/2½ cups Chicken Stock (see page 180)
600ml/1pint/2½ cups Beef Stock (see page 180)
salt
2 tbsp snipped chives or whole flat leaf parsley leaves, to garnish

FOR THE TORTELLINI

100g/3½oz Ravioli Dough (see page 186)
1 egg, lightly beaten
100g/3½oz/scant ½ cup mascarpone cheese
20g/¾oz truffle, finely chopped
1 drop of truffle oil

To make the clarification: In a large pan, mix together the beef, chicken, chopped vegetables, tomato purée (paste), chopped tomatoes, thyme, bay leaf and peppercorns. Add the egg whites and mix in well, then add the cold stocks and mix again. Season with salt, set over a low heat, and stir frequently until the clarification begins to rise to the surface. Simmer gently for 1½ hours, then pass the consommé through a sieve lined with muslin (cheesecloth).

To make the tortellini: Roll out the dough on the thinnest setting of a pasta machine. Cut the pasta into 4cm/1½ in squares and brush with the beaten egg. Mix the mascarpone, truffle and truffle oil. Divide the mascarpone mixture into 20 and put a piece in the middle of each pasta square. Fold over the squares from corner to corner, then wrap the corners around your index finger and press both ends together.

Cook the tortellini in plenty of well-salted, boiling water or, even better, well-seasoned stock for about 3 minutes.

To serve, place 2 or 3 tortellini in each soup bowl, add the hot consommé, and sprinkle on the snipped chives or parsley leaves.

Langoustines with Goose Liver and Mango Carpaccio

This most elegant appetizer is a very delicate dish, which benefits from a robust and peppery sauce, offset by the sweetness of the mango. These quite different ingredients sound an unlikely combination, but, as happens so often with food, when you eat the dish, you will find that they create a superb harmony.

SERVES 4

1 ripe mango
8 x 50g/2oz slices of fried goose liver
8 langoustines, shelled,
100ml/3½fl oz/scant ½ cup Pepper Sauce (see page 184)
50ml/2fl oz/¼ cup Salsa Verde (see page 184)
sea salt and freshly ground pepper
4 chervil sprigs, to garnish

Peel the mango and slice it very thinly, then cut out 24 x 4cm/1½in rounds from the slices and place them on each plate. Season the goose liver, place in a non-stick frying pan (skillet) and fry quickly on for 30 seconds on each side. Remove the goose liver, leaving the fat in the pan, and keep warm. Season the langoustines and fry them in the goose liver fat for 30 seconds on each side.
To serve, place 2 pieces of goose liver and 2 langoustines decoratively on the mango discs. Pour a little pepper sauce around and on top, and do the same with the salsa verde. Garnish with a sprig of chervil.

Lobster Ravioli in Saffron Broth

This is a dish that just sells and sells at The Savoy; it's luxurious and everybody seems to like lobster in any guise. It can as easily be done with just white fish. The seafood broth goes well with other fish dishes, or simply on its own as a light soup.

SERVES 4

FOR THE LOBSTER FILLING

1 x 500g/1lb 2oz live lobster
100g/3½oz white fish trimmings
1 egg white
300ml/10fl oz/1¼ cups double (heavy) cream
salt and cayenne pepper

200g/7oz Ravioli Dough (see page 186)
eggwash (1 egg yolk, beaten with 1 tbsp milk)
400ml/14fl oz/1¾ cups Seafood Broth (see page 181)
2 tbsp snipped chives
1 tomato, peeled, de-seeded and diced
50g/2oz brown shrimps
a little oscietra caviar (optional)

To prepare the lobster filling: Drop the lobster into salted, boiling water for 2 minutes, then drain and cool in iced water. Remove the shells and keep them for another use. Cut the claws in half lengthways and reserve.

Mince (grind) the lobster tail and the fish trimmings through the fine plate of a mincer (grinder), or pulse them very quickly in a food processor in short bursts so as not to overheat the mixture. Pass the mixture through a fine drum sieve into a bowl, and set it on ice.

Gradually stir in the egg white, then the cream. Season with salt and cayenne pepper and chill. The mousse should be as light as possible; it will firm up in the refrigerator, so add a little more cream when you take it out.

To make the ravioli: Roll out the dough on the thinnest setting of a pasta machine. Cut it into 8 rounds. Place 80g/3oz of lobster mousse on one round of dough and brush some eggwash around it. Top with another round of dough and press it around the lobster filling to make a ravioli shape about 8cm/3¼in diameter. Cut this out with a 9cm/3½in pastry (cookie) cutter. Make 3 more ravioli in this way.

Bring a pan of salted water to the boil, put in the ravioli and simmer for about 5 minutes.

To serve: Heat the seafood broth and finish it with egg yolk and cream, as in the recipe on page 181. Add the chives, tomatoes and brown shrimp, then the lobster claws, and heat gently for about 30 seconds.

Put the ravioli in soup bowls, pour on the seafood broth and place a halved lobster claw on top of the ravioli. Top with a little caviar if you wish.

Parmesan-crusted Poached Eggs on Creamed Spinach with White Alba Truffles

White truffles from Alba are the most expensive of all, but for me they have an incomparable flavour and an overpowering, earthy smell with a strong whiff of garlic. This dish helps to bring out the flavour, which is further enhanced if you store the eggs overnight in the same container as the truffle. Its aroma permeates the eggshells and deepens the experience. This dish is certainly not something you might eat every day, but it is one that you must eat at least once in your life.

SERVES 4

150ml/5fl oz/⅔ cup white wine vinegar
4 organic eggs
40g/1½oz/⅓ cup plain (all-purpose) flour
1 egg, lightly beaten
100g/3½oz/1¾ cups fresh white breadcrumbs
100g/3½oz/generous 1 cup freshly grated Parmesan
oil, for deep-frying
200g/7oz baby spinach
100ml/3½fl oz/scant ½ cup double (heavy) cream
freshly grated nutmeg
40g/1½oz fresh white Alba truffle
salt and freshly ground pepper

Pour 400ml/14fl oz/1¾ cups water and two-thirds of the vinegar into a wide, shallow pan, bring to the boil, then reduce to a simmer. Do not add salt, as it would destroy the protein in the egg white and spoil the shape of the poached egg.

Crack an egg into a cup, and slide it into the simmering water. Repeat with the other 3 eggs; you will probably be able to fit all four into the pan at once. If not, cook in two batches. Simmer the eggs for 3–4 minutes, until the whites have set around the yolks. Remove with a slotted spoon and cool in iced water and remaining vinegar. Dry on kitchen paper (paper towels) and season with salt and pepper.

Put the flour on a plate and the beaten egg in another. Turn the poached eggs in the flour, then in the beaten egg to coat lightly. Mix the breadcrumbs with the Parmesan, then turn the eggs in the mixture to coat them evenly.

Heat the oil to 150°C/300°F. Meanwhile, blanch the spinach in salted, boiling water for 1 minute, refresh in iced water and squeeze out all the water.

In a pan, boil the double (heavy) cream to reduce it by half. Add the chopped spinach and season with salt, pepper and a little grated nutmeg (be careful not to overdo the nutmeg, as it is very strong).

Gently place the Parmesan-crusted eggs in the hot oil and fry for not more than 1½ minutes, until golden brown. Do not overcook; the yolks must still be runny.

Divide the spinach among 4 plates, and top with the eggs. Using a truffle shaver or fine vegetable peeler, shave the truffle evenly on to the eggs or spinach, and serve immediately.

Fillets of John Dory with Herb Sauce

This springtime dish is very light and refreshing. It can be served as an appetizer or a main dish (in which case, allow 150g/5oz fish per person). If John Dory is hard to find, you could use sea bass or hake fillets instead.

SERVES 4 AS AN APPETIZER

½ onion, finely chopped
100ml/3½fl oz/scant ½ cup olive oil
1 garlic clove, crushed
1 fennel bulb, peeled and cut into 1cm/½in slices
200ml/7fl oz/scant 1 cup Chicken Stock (see page 180)
1 tbsp freshly grated Parmesan cheese
4 x 100g/3½oz John Dory fillets, unskinned
juice of ½ lemon
salt and freshly ground pepper

FOR THE HERB SAUCE

2 tbsp unsalted (sweet) butter
3 tbsp mixed olives, stoned (pitted)
2 tbsp chopped fresh herbs (chives, flat parsley, tarragon
  and chervil)

FOR THE GARNISH

2 handfuls of Herb Salad (see recipe right)
2 tbsp Lemon Dressing (see page 182)

Heat the grill (broiler) and heat the oven to 200°C/400°F/Gas Mark 6.
To cook the fennel: In a pan, gently fry the onion in a little olive oil until soft and translucent, add the garlic and sweat for another minute. Add the fennel and chicken stock, season with salt and pepper, and simmer until tender. Transfer the fennel to a gratin dish and sprinkle with the Parmesan. Place under the grill until the cheese has melted. Set aside. Reserve the cooking stock to use for a soup – it is delicious.
Heat a non-stick frying pan (skillet) and add a little oil. Season the fish fillets with salt and pepper, put them in the pan skin side down and place a small, light plate on top to prevent them from curling. Sear until the skin is very crispy. Turn the fish over and add the lemon juice. Caramelize over high heat until all the lemon juice has evaporated, then transfer the fish to an ovenproof dish and cook in the oven for 2 minutes.

To make the sauce: Put the remaining oil, the butter, olives and herbs in a blender and blend until smooth.
To serve: Place a slice of fennel on each plate, top with a John Dory fillet, and pour a little of the sauce around it. Toss the herb salad in the lemon dressing and arrange it on top of the fish.

HERB SALAD

1 tbsp white wine vinegar
1 tbsp lime juice
2 tbsp extra virgin olive oil
15g/½oz/½ cup chervil
15g/½oz/½ cup chives, cut into 1cm/½in lengths
2 tbsp basil leaves
a few dill sprigs
50g/2oz/2 cups celery leaves, chopped
4 tbsp rocket (arugula)
salt and freshly ground pepper

Make a dressing with the vinegar, lime juice and olive oil.
Toss all the herbs in the dressing and adjust the seasoning.

Seared Scallops and Sweetbreads in Lemon and Thyme Reduction

I think this marriage of seafood and offal (variety meats) is made in heaven, as this wonderful dinner appetizer proves. As in many marriages, the dish is full of opposites that work together most harmoniously, and the lemon and thyme reduction helps to bring out the flavours of the scallops and sweetbreads.

SERVES 4

300g/11oz Maris Piper potatoes, unpeeled
2 tbsp olive oil
200g/7oz sweetbreads, blanched and cut into 4 slices
  (see preparation note below)
50g/2oz/½ cup plain (all-purpose) flour
100g/3½oz/scant ½ cup unsalted (sweet) butter
4 prepared scallops (about 40g/1½oz each)
4 thyme sprigs, plus extra to garnish
2 tbsp lemon juice
200ml/7fl oz/scant 1 cup Chicken Stock (see page 180)
handful of Radish Salad (see page 188)
a little Lemon Dressing (see page 182)
salt and freshly ground pepper

Boil the potatoes for about 20 minutes until half-cooked and leave to cool. Peel and grate them and season with salt and pepper.
To make the potato rounds: Place a 10cm/4in pastry (cookie) cutter in a large non-stick frying pan (skillet) with a touch of olive oil, put in a 5mm/¼in layer of grated potato, and press down gently. Repeat to make 3 more potato rounds. Fry very quickly over high heat, turning the potatoes once, until golden brown and crispy on both sides. Keep warm.
Season the sweetbreads, dust lightly with flour, and fry in a little butter and oil for about 1 minute on each side until golden. Season the scallops, put them in the pan with the thyme and a little butter and oil, and fry for about 30 seconds on each side. Make sure they are still opaque inside. Take the scallops and sweetbreads out of the pan.
To make the lemon and thyme reduction: Remove the thyme sprigs from the pan, pour away the fat, add ½ teaspoon lemon juice and reduce completely. Turn the scallops in this reduction a couple of times, then remove them. Add the remaining lemon juice to the pan, reduce it completely, then add the chicken stock and pinch of thyme leaves. Reduce slightly, add the remaining butter, and blend with a hand-held blender until the reduction becomes almost white. Season with salt and pepper.

To serve: Toss the radish salad in a little lemon dressing. Put a potato round on each plate and top with a slice of sweetbread and a scallop. Put a sprig of thyme in the sweetbreads, pour a little of the lemon and thyme reduction over and around it, and garnish with the radish salad.

TO BLANCH SWEETBREADS

Put the sweetbreads under cold running water for 3 hours. Remove all the white membrane and fat. Blanch the sweetbreads in chicken stock with an onion stuck with 2 cloves and a bay leaf, and seasoning. When the liquid starts simmering, cook for about 12 minutes.
Leave the sweetbreads to cool in the stock. Once cooled, remove them, place between two plates and put a light weight on top. Leave in the refrigerator for 2–2½ hours.

Party Time at The Savoy

The Savoy has always been the ultimate venue for parties and celebrations. From Shakespeare's quatercentenary to the premières of Harry Potter films, the Banqueting Department can provide whatever is required.

Their biggest challenge was the Gondola party thrown by American billionaire George Kessler in 1905 to celebrate his birthday. The scene was Venice; painted backdrops of palazzi surrounded the courtyard, which was flooded to make a "lagoon". The water was dyed blue, and a flock of swans was set to swim on it. (Unfortunately, the dye poisoned the swans, who expired and had to be hastily removed.) Twenty-four guests dined in a silk-lined gondola to the strains of a band playing in another. After dinner, the Great Caruso serenaded the assembled company with operatic arias. The grand finale was a huge birthday cake, borne in on the back of a baby elephant.

The ball of the century was held to celebrate the Queen's coronation on 2 June, 1953. Designed by Cecil Beaton and Bridget d'Oyly Carte, the Restaurant was transformed into an Elizabethan pavilion, tented with miles of billowing silk and decorated with ostrich feather coronets and yards of topiary peacock hedges. The ballroom entrance was hung with fake ermine curtains and all the doors were covered in studded red velvet. Yeoman from the Tower of London formed the guard of honour to welcome the 1500 guests – royalty from around the globe, great statesmen and glamorous stars of stage and screen. After a magnificent dinner, there was dancing to four bands and an abundance of pipers from the Royal regiments. Exuberant guests climbed up to the roof to watch the fireworks exploding over the Thames. At midnight, Elizabethan party ruffs and hats cascaded from the ceiling, and the star-studded cabaret included Noel Coward and Maurice Chevalier.

For The Savoy's own centenary, Anton Edelmann created a superb five-course banquet based on the recipes of Escoffier. Of course there followed another magnificent ball, culminating in a spectacular firework display that set the Thames alight once more.

There's no shortage of surprises at Savoy parties. Perhaps you require a perfectly pink party, complete with live flamingos? It has been done. Film premières, weddings, birthdays, launch parties – all are grist to The Savoy's mill. Agatha Christie's almost immortal *The Mousetrap* celebrated its tenth anniversary here, with a birthday cake weighing half a ton. For a horror movie première, the ballroom was transformed into Dracula's Den. Not all the guests at such events are welcome; showman Billy Butlin once brought his pet leopard to a circus-opening party. His "guest" was shown the door.

Today's celebrations tend to be less dramatic, but The Savoy is still *the* place to throw a party. The Wimbledon Champions' Ball, the annual Evening Standard Drama and Film Awards, weddings, bar mitzvahs, celebrations of every kind … The Savoy is proud to host them all.

Seared Red Mullet with Scallops, Crushed New Potatoes and Salsa Verde

A whole small red mullet is just the right size for a main course at dinner. This simple dish is popular with our health-conscious guests, as it is light and low in calories, but bursting with flavour. I love the combination of the sweetness of the scallops, the delicate flavour of the red mullet and the tangy sauce. If you can't find red mullet, small snapper makes a good substitute.

SERVES 4

4 small red mullet or snapper (about 200g/7oz each),
  scaled and cleaned
2 tbsp olive oil
½ lemon
25g/1oz/2 tbsp unsalted (sweet) butter
4 large scallops, halved horizontally
sea salt and freshly ground black pepper

FOR THE GARNISH

20g/2oz/½ cup black olives, stoned (pitted) and finely chopped
1 tbsp finely snipped chives
2 plum tomatoes, peeled, de-seeded and finely diced
50g/2oz baby courgettes (zucchini), sliced and boiled
1 tbsp parsley leaves
50g/2 oz/generous ⅓ cup broad (fava) beans, shelled
125ml/4fl oz/½ cup Salsa Verde (see page 184)

FOR THE CRUSHED POTATOES

450g/1lb medium-sized waxy new potatoes
15g/½oz/1 tbsp unsalted (sweet) butter
2 tbsp balsamic vinegar
1 tbsp chopped black olives
2 tbsp olive oil
salt

To make the crushed potatoes: Put the potatoes in a pan of cold salted water, bring to the boil and simmer until tender. Drain the potatoes, then crush gently with the back of a fork and mix in butter, balsamic vinegar, chopped olives and olive oil. Season with salt and pepper and keep warm.

Heat a cast-iron ridged griddle pan and heat the oven to 200°C/400°F/Gas Mark 6. Season the fish with sea salt and pepper and coat them with a little of the oil. Place on the hot griddle pan and leave for 1 minute to sear and start to cook. Turn them over and cook for another 4 minutes. Squeeze a little lemon juice over the fish, remove them from the pan and transfer to a roasting tray (pan). Cook in the oven until opaque.

To serve: Divide the crushed potatoes among the middles of four plates, and top with a fish and 2 scallop halves. Sprinkle the olives, chives, diced tomatoes, courgettes (zucchini), parsley leaves and broad (fava) beans on top. Finish with a drizzle of salsa verde.

New Season's Welsh Lamb with Crushed Baked Potatoes and Pak Choi (Bok Choy)

This is a very robust and flavoursome dish which Savoy chefs serve in spring when the new season's lamb is at its best. Rump is a delicious cut of meat, but it is often not appreciated and is therefore very good value. For added zing, the mint pesto could be spiced up with a little chilli.

SERVES 4

500g/1lb 2oz Maris Piper baking potatoes, scrubbed
200ml/7fl oz/scant 1 cup olive oil
2 tbsp chopped chives
50g/2oz/½ cup black olives, stoned (pitted) and chopped
4 rumps (rounds) of new season's lamb
4 heads of pak choi (bok choy)
2 tsp chilli oil
200ml/7fl oz/scant 1 cup Mint Pesto (see page 183)
salt and freshly ground pepper

To make the crushed potatoes: Heat the oven to 220°C/425°F/ Gas Mark 7. Put in the potatoes and bake for about 1 hour until soft. When they are cool enough to handle, peel them and crush with the back of a fork. Mix in all but 1 tsp of the olive oil, the chives and black olives, and season with salt and pepper. Cover and keep warm.

Season the lamb with salt and pepper. Heat a deep frying pan (skillet) and add a film of oil. Put in the lamb and turn it in the pan until it is sealed on both sides. Transfer the rumps (rounds) to a baking tray (cookie sheet), put them in the hot oven and roast for 12 minutes. The lamb will be medium-rare. Take it out of the oven, leave it to rest for 10 minutes, then cut each rump on the bias into 3 or 4 slices.

Remove the outside leaves from the pak choi (bok choy) and trim the end of the stalks. Bring a pan of salted water to the boil, put in the pak choi and blanch for 3 minutes. Refresh in iced water and drain.

Heat the chilli oil in a deep frying pan (skillet) and add the pak choi. Season. Turn the pak choi in the oil until hot, then place 1 on each plate. Neatly pile the crushed potatoes on the side, arrange the slices of lamb and sprinkle some warm mint pesto on top of the lamb or on the side.

Slow-braised and Flash-fried Scottish Beef on Spicy Bean Stew

I really like this combination of two cooking methods and two completely different pieces of meat. The oxtail provides the strong yet subtle flavours of a working muscle, and produces a superb sauce, which contrasts wonderfully well with the rare, tender fillet (tenderloin). The spicy bean stew rounds off this robust winter dinners dish.

I can bone an oxtail in 12 minutes (although my colleague Gary can do it in 9½ minutes flat!), but if the prospect seems too daunting, cut it into pieces at the joints, leave it on the bone, and omit the chicken mousse altogether – but the dish won't be quite so good of course.

SERVES 4

FOR THE CHICKEN MOUSSE

100g/3½oz chicken breast portion, skinned and boned
1 egg white
100ml/3½fl oz/scant ½ cup double (heavy) cream
1 oxtail, boned
50ml/2fl oz/¼ cup oil
100g/3½oz roasting vegetables (1 peeled onion, 1 peeled carrot, 1 celery stalk, white part of ¼ leek, outside leaves removed), cut into large pieces
2 tbsp tomato purée (paste)
½ tsp black peppercorns
200ml/7fl oz/scant 1 cup red wine
2 tbsp plain (all-purpose) flour
900ml/1½ pints/3¾ cups Chicken Stock (see page 180)
1 thyme sprig
1 marjoram sprig
4 x 80g/3oz pieces of beef fillet (tenderloin), trimmed
100g/3½oz/¾ cup shelled broad (fava) beans
50g/2oz green beans, cooked al dente and halved
40g/1½oz/scant ¼ cup unsalted (sweet) butter
1 tomato, peeled, de-seeded and diced
salt and freshly ground pepper

FOR THE SPICY BEAN STEW

1 onion, chopped
4 garlic cloves, crushed
½ chilli, de-seeded and chopped
2 rashers (slices) of smoked bacon
100g/3½oz/generous ½ cup white haricot (navy) beans, soaked for 1 hour
salt and freshly ground pepper

To make the chicken mousse: Whizz the chicken in a food processor until smooth and season with salt and pepper. Place in a bowl over ice and cool. Add the egg white in small amounts and mix well, then add the cream in small amounts and mix well. Spread half the boned oxtail with the chicken mousse and fold over the other half to enclose it. Tie securely with kitchen string at 2cm/¾in intervals.

To cook the oxtail: Heat the oven to 140°C/275°F/Gas Mark 1. Heat a little oil in a flameproof casserole about the size of the oxtail, season the oxtail, place in the casserole and colour it all over. Remove the oxtail, put the roasting vegetables in the casserole and colour, then add the tomato purée (paste) and the peppercorns. Caramelize the tomato purée (paste) for 2 minutes, then add a little red wine, bring to the boil, and reduce to a thick glaze. Repeat with the remaining wine, adding it in 2 batches. When the last of the wine has been reduced to a glaze, sift in the flour and stir well for 1 minute.

Gradually add 300ml/10fl oz/1¼ cups of the chicken stock and season with salt and pepper. Add the herbs, then the oxtail, bring to the boil, put on the lid and braise in the oven for about 3½ hours until tender, turning the oxtail every 30 minutes or so. If the liquid evaporates, add more chicken stock.

Transfer the oxtail to a dish and pass the sauce through a fine sieve. Reduce it if it seems too thin and pour it over the oxtail.

To make the spicy bean stew: In a pan, sweat the chopped onion in a little oil until soft and translucent. Add the garlic and chilli, and sweat for another minute. Add the bacon and sweat until slightly crispy. Drain the haricot (navy) beans and add them to the pan. Pour in enough chicken stock to cover the beans and simmer very gently, stirring occasionally, until the beans are very tender and most of the liquid has evaporated. If it evaporates completely, add more chicken stock. Season with salt and pepper.

Season the beef fillets (tenderloin) and fry in a little oil until rare. Heat the broad (fava) beans and green beans in a little butter and season, then add the diced tomato at the last moment.

To serve: Spoon some bean stew on to each plate. Cut a 1.5cm/½in thick slice of oxtail and place on it top. Cut each beef fillet in half at an angle and arrange on top of the oxtail. Pour a little sauce over and sprinkle the vegetables over and around the dish.

Salmon Trout "en Gondole"

In 1905, the champagne millionaire George A. Kessler gave himself a splendiferous birthday party at The Savoy (described on page 99). Inspired by reports of this amazing occasion, my predecessor at The Savoy, Silvino Trompetto, came up with this recipe for *Truite Salmonée en Gondole*, and it still featured on the menu when I started working at the hotel in 1982. One of the great classics, it is a spectacular looking dish, and most enjoyable to eat, but before you embark on it, I strongly advise you to ask your fishmonger (fish store) to bone out the salmon trout from the back so it opens like a butterfly.

SERVES 6

1 x 2.5kg/5½lb salmon trout, ungutted
butter, for greasing
200ml/7fl oz/scant 1 cup white wine
500ml/18fl oz/2¼ cups Fish Stock (see page 180)
salt, freshly ground pepper and cayenne pepper

FOR THE SAUCE

50g/2oz shallots, finely chopped
2 star anise
pinch of saffron threads
½ tsp black peppercorns, crushed
50ml/2fl oz/¼ cup white wine vinegar
200ml/7fl oz/scant 1 cup white wine
400ml/14fl oz/1¾ cups double (heavy) cream

FOR THE GARNISH

120g/4oz fillet of sole or similar white fish, skinned
50g/2oz/½ cup plain (all-purpose) flour
2 eggs, lightly beaten
50g/2oz/1 cup fresh white breadcrumbs
50g/2oz/¼ cup butter
6 small button (white) mushrooms, washed
2 tbsp white wine
100g/3½oz fish mousse
6 puff pastry fleurons (see recipe right)

If you feel you should bone and butterfly the fish yourself, this is how it's done. Open the salmon trout by cutting carefully down either side of the spine. Remove the backbone with scissors without damaging the head, tail or belly of the fish. Discard the intestines and wash the body cavity thoroughly. Pull out the small bones with tweezers and dry the fish with a kitchen cloth.

To cook: Heat the oven to 180°C/350°F/Gas Mark 4. Place the fish in a buttered ovenproof dish, season with salt and pepper and pour over half the wine and all the seasoned fish stock. Cover with foil and poach in the oven for 12 minutes.

Meanwhile, make the sauce reduction: Put the shallots, star anise, saffron, crushed peppercorns and white wine vinegar in a pan, and reduce completely. Add the white wine and reduce to a thick syrupy glaze.

When the fish is cooked, remove it from the cooking juices and keep it warm. Add the juices to the sauce reduction and reduce the reduction by three-quarters. Add the cream and reduce until slightly thickened. Season with salt and cayenne pepper and pass through a fine sieve.

To prepare the garnishes: Cut the sole fillets into long strips, season and turn them first in flour, then egg and lastly in the breadcrumbs. Heat the oil to 160°C/320°F, add the sole and deep-fry in the hot oil until golden.

Heat a little butter in a small pan, add the mushrooms and sweat for 1 minute. Add the white wine, cover, and cook for 2 minutes.

Using 2 teaspoons, shape the fish mousse into 6 small quenelles and place in a heatproof dish. Cover with boiling salted water and simmer for 3 minutes until cooked. Drain on kitchen paper (paper towels).

To serve: Place the salmon trout on a large dish, and garnish with the fish quenelles and mushrooms. Pour the sauce all over and arrange the fish strips on top like ribs. Surround the fish with the puff pastry fleurons.

PUFF PASTRY FLEURONS

40g/1½oz Puff Pastry (see page 186)
1 egg yolk, beaten
poppy seeds
sesame seeds

Roll out the puff pastry to a thickness of 3mm/⅛in, making sure to roll it in different directions to prevent distortion during cooking. Using a 6cm/2½in fluted pastry (cookie) cutter, stamp out 4 crescent-shaped pieces. Place on a buttered baking tray (cookie sheet), brush the tops with egg yolk and sprinkle with a few poppy and sesame seeds. Leave to rest in the refrigerator for 20 minutes, then bake in a heated oven at 200°C/400°F/Gas Mark 6 for 15 minutes until golden brown.

Venison Fillet on Baked Beetroot (Beet) with Sage Stuffing

Venison is widely available nowadays, and is really never tough, unlike in the old days. It is a very lean meat and therefore very low in cholesterol. Like most game, it can withstand a strong, gutsy sauce like the peppery version served in the River Restaurant.

SERVES 4

2 large beetroot (beets)
2 tbsp olive oil

FOR THE SAGE STUFFING

50g/2oz onions, finely chopped
1 garlic clove, crushed
50g/2oz streaky (fatty) bacon, finely chopped
50g/2oz button (white) mushrooms, finely chopped
100g/3½oz chicken livers
200g/7oz/3½ cups breadcrumbs
15g/½oz/½ cup sage, chopped
4 tsp Chicken Stock (see page 180)

FOR THE PEA AND BROCCOLI PURÉE

50g/2oz onions, finely chopped
1 garlic clove, crushed
1 potato, peeled and diced
50ml/2fl oz/¼ cup double (heavy) cream
600g/1¼lb/5 cups frozen peas
150g/5oz broccoli
pinch of ground nutmeg

4 x 120g/4oz venison fillets, cut from the saddle, all skin removed
200ml/7fl oz/scant 1 cup Peppery Game Sauce (see recipe right)
salt and freshly ground pepper

To cook the beetroot (beets): Heat the oven to 200°C/400°F/Gas Mark 6. Wrap the beetroot with a few drops of olive oil in foil and bake in the oven for about 1 hour until very soft. Keep warm. Meanwhile, make the sage stuffing. Put half the onions and half the garlic in a pan with a little olive oil, and sweat slowly until soft and translucent. Add the bacon and mushrooms and sweat until soft, then add the chicken livers and season with salt and pepper. Sweat for a further 3 minutes, then add the breadcrumbs, sage and chicken stock, and cook for 1 more minute. Using a hand-held blender, blend the contents of the pan until completely smooth. Adjust the seasoning.

To make the pea and broccoli purée: In a pan, sweat the remaining onions and garlic in a little oil until soft. Add the potato and cream, cover the pan and cook until soft. Add the peas and broccoli, and simmer until the cream is well reduced. Blend with a hand-held blender, and season with salt, pepper and nutmeg.

To cook the venison: Heat the oven to 220°C/425°F/Gas Mark 7. Season the fillets. Heat the remaining oil in a frying pan (skillet) and quickly seal the venison on both sides. Place on a baking tray (cookie sheet) and bake in the hot oven for 6 minutes until cooked medium. Leave to rest for 5 minutes in a warm place.

Peel and slice the beetroot (beets) and arrange them on the plates. Slice the venison and place on top. Shape the sage stuffing into quenelles, and place a quenelle of stuffing and a quenelle of pea and broccoli purée next to the venison. Pour the sauce over.

PEPPERY GAME SAUCE

MAKES ABOUT 1 LITRE/1¾PINTS/4 CUPS

2 tbsp oil
200g/7oz venison bones and trimmings
1 onion, chopped
1 carrot, chopped
½ leek, outside leaves discarded, washed and chopped
2 celery stalks, chopped
½ tbsp tomato purée (paste)
100ml/3½fl oz/scant ½ cup red wine
850ml/1½pints/3¾ cups Chicken Stock (see page 180)
½ tbsp black peppercorns, crushed
thyme sprig
1 tsp juniper berries
1 tbsp redcurrant jelly
salt

Heat the oven to 220°C/425°F/Gas Mark 7. Heat a little oil in a roasting tin (pan) and add the venison bones and trimmings. Roast in the oven until browned, stirring occasionally.

Add the vegetables and roast for a further 10 minutes.

Put the roasting tin on the hob (stovetop), add the tomato purée (paste), then pour in half the red wine and reduce by half. Add the remaining wine and reduce again by half. Add the chicken stock, peppercorns, thyme and juniper berries. Simmer for 45 minutes, skimming and stirring frequently.

Pass the sauce through a fine sieve back into the pan and reduce by half. Stir in the redcurrant jelly and season with salt.

Grilled Ribs of Beef with
Warm Red (Bell) Pepper Chutney

The quality of meat in this recipe is of paramount importance.
Paired with the chutney, it is a winning formula.

SERVES 4

2 x 400g/14oz ribs of beef, cut off the sirloin
1 tbsp groundnut (peanut) oil
20g/¾oz/1½ tbsp unsalted (sweet) butter
2 rosemary sprigs
salt and freshly ground black pepper

FOR THE CHUTNEY

4 red (bell) peppers
2 tbsp groundnut (peanut) oil
1 red onion, finely chopped
1 garlic clove, finely chopped
1 red chilli, de-seeded and finely diced
1 tsp sugar
2 tbsp red wine vinegar
200ml/7fl oz/scant 1 cup Chicken Stock (see page 180)
4 plum tomatoes, peeled, de-seeded and diced

To make the chutney: Put the red (bell) peppers under a very hot
grill (broiler) until blistered and well charred all over. Place in a
plastic bag and leave until cool enough to handle, then peel,
de-seed and cut into 1cm/½ in squares.
Heat the groundnut oil in a frying pan (skillet), put in the onion,
and sweat until soft. Add the garlic and sweat for another minute.
Add the diced peppers, chilli and sugar, and sweat for a further
2 minutes. Pour in the red wine vinegar and boil until reduced by
half. Stir in the chicken stock, reduce the heat and simmer until the
chutney is very thick. Add the tomatoes and cook for 3 minutes,
stirring frequently. Keep the chutney warm.
To cook the beef: Heat the oven to 220°C/425°F/Gas Mark 7.
Heat the grill (broiler) to hot. Season the beef ribs with salt and
pepper. Turn them in the oil to coat, and cook under the hot grill
for 2 minutes on each side. Place in the oven for 15 minutes. They
will be medium rare. Adjust the cooking time down or up if you
prefer your beef rare or well done. Leave to rest in a warm place
for 15 minutes.
Collect all the juices that have seeped out of the meat. Cut the
beef across the grain in to 1cm/½in slices. Melt the butter in
a small pan, add the rosemary, and heat gently until the butter is
golden brown. Pour it over the beef. Add the meat juices to the
chutney and serve with the beef.

Mille-feuilles of Mushrooms with Artichokes and Tarragon

A very summery vegetarian dish, light and seasonal. A nice idea is to change the vegetables with the seasons.

4 sheets of brik or filo pastry
100ml/3½fl oz/scant ½ cup olive oil
50g/2oz/¼ cup unsalted (sweet) butter
1 egg yolk, lightly beaten
25g/1oz/1 cup fresh tarragon
4 artichoke bottoms
200g/7oz mixed wild mushrooms (eg: ceps, chanterelles, girolles, black trumpets)
100g/3½oz button (white) mushrooms
juice of ½ lemon
50ml/2fl oz/¼ cup white wine
50ml/2fl oz/¼ cup double (heavy) cream
50ml/2fl oz/¼ cup Madeira
1 shallot, finely chopped
1 garlic clove, crushed
40g/1½oz slow-roasted tomatoes
salt and freshly ground pepper

To prepare the pastry: Using an 8cm/3½in pastry (cookie) cutter, cut 4 rounds out of each sheet of brik or filo. Heat ½ tsp each of oil and butter in a non-stick frying pan (skillet), put in 8 of the pastry rounds, and fry until lightly browned (they will become darker over time, so do not leave them too long in the pan at this stage). Drain on kitchen paper (paper towels).
Lay 4 of the remaining pastry rounds on a table and brush with egg yolk. Put 3 tarragon leaves on each one and top with the remaining rounds. Fry as before and drain on kitchen paper.
To prepare the artichoke bottoms: Break off the artichoke stalks. Pull off the larger outside leaves, then cut off all the smaller leaves with a sharp knife. When you reach the hairy choke, scoop it out with a teaspoon. Trim any remaining leaf or stalk from the artichoke bottoms and cut each one into quarters. Rub all over with the lemon half to prevent discoloration.
To make the filling: Cut the artichoke bottoms into 5mm/1¼in strips. Trim the wild mushrooms and blanch quickly in salted, boiling water. Drain and reserve.

To make the sauce: In a pan, sweat the button (white) mushrooms in a little butter, season with salt and pepper, add the lemon juice and white wine, cover and cook for 2 minutes. Remove the mushrooms and reduce the liquid to a syrupy consistency. Add the cream and reduce by half, then add the Madeira, and adjust the seasoning.
Sweat the shallot in 1 tsp olive oil until soft and translucent; add the garlic and sweat for another minute, then add the wild mushrooms and season with salt and pepper. Toss the sliced artichokes in a little butter and season. Add the slow-roasted tomatoes.
To assemble the mille-feuilles: Place a single pastry round on each plate and arrange some of the artichokes on top. Top with a second single pastry round, divide the wild mushrooms among them, then top each mille-feuille with a double tarragon-filled pastry round. Chop the remaining tarragon, stir it into the sauce, and pour a little sauce around the mille-feuilles.

Calves' Liver with Chervil Root Purée and Pancetta

In terms of flavour, I think chervil must be the most useless herb, yet I and many other chefs use tons of it, because its beautiful appearance is hard to beat. Chervil root, however, is one of the tastiest and most refined of all aromatics. It is still a well-kept secret in Britain, where it is hardly ever used, but in France it has always been regarded as a delicacy. It is best used as a purée, is very easy to prepare, and has a most unusual and explosive flavour. The season for fresh chervil is very short, from the end of autumn (fall) to just before Christmas, and the flavour is best after the first frosts have set in. It goes very well with game and offal (variety meats).

SERVES 4

500g/1lb 2oz chervil root, peeled
200ml/7fl oz/scant 1 cup milk
100ml/3½fl oz/scant ½ cup double (heavy) cream
16 button (pearl) onions, peeled
15g/½oz/½ cup thyme (reserve 4 sprigs for the garnish)
2 tbsp oil
1 apple, peeled, cored and cut into 5mm/¼in slices
4 x 135g/4½oz slices of calves' liver
4 thin slices of pancetta, dried (see Poached Eggs on Smoked
  Haddock and Toasted English Muffins, page 142)
salt and freshly ground pepper

To make the chervil root purée: Cut the chervil root into even-sized pieces. Place in a pan and cover with the milk and an equal quantity of water. Season with salt and simmer until tender. Drain and rub through a fine sieve or vegetable mill. Add the cream, season with salt and pepper, and keep warm.

Place the onions and the thyme in a pan just big enough to hold them in a single layer, add a little oil and cook over high heat until well coloured all over. Take the pan off the heat and cover; the onions will soften in about 5 minutes.

In a non-stick frying pan (skillet), heat a film of oil, add the apple slices and fry quickly on both sides until lightly coloured.

Heat a griddle pan until very hot. Season the liver, put it in the pan, and cook on both sides until done to your liking.

Divide the chervil root purée among the plates. Stick the dried pancetta in it, and put a slice of liver beside it. Top with the apple and onions, and garnish with a sprig of thyme.

Classic Lobster Thermidor
with Wild Rice

Of all the many ways of cooking lobster, Thermidor is the dish that has made the biggest impact over the last century. Created by the great Escoffier in the late nineteenth century, there was a time when it featured on almost every restaurant menu. Nowadays, it has virtually disappeared, but occasionally I cook it and, every time I do, am struck by how well it works and how delicious it tastes. As the combination of flavours is spot on.

SERVES 4

4 x 500g/1lb 2oz live lobsters (preferably Scottish)
100ml/3½fl oz/scant ½ cup white wine
1 shallot, finely chopped
½ tsp crushed black peppercorns
1 star anise
300ml/10fl oz/1¼ cups Fish Stock (see page 180)
400ml/14fl oz/1¾ cups double (heavy) cream
½ tsp Dijon mustard
4 tsp shredded flat parsley leaves
1 tbsp Hollandaise Sauce (see page 183)
salt and freshly ground pepper
225g/8oz/1 cup Wild Rice Mix (see recipe right), to serve

To cook the lobsters: Bring a large pan of water to the boil, plunge in the lobsters, and cook for 5 minutes. Drain and refresh in cold water.
To remove the shells: Twist off the two large claws, then twist them at the first joint to separate them from the knuckle. Tap both ends on the work surface (counter) to loosen the flesh. Break off the small pincer claws and ease out the flesh. Using a sharp knife, carefully cut away the side of the shell, then crack the large claws around the middle, and carefully pull apart to release the flesh. Cut the lobsters in half lengthways and remove the stomach sacs from the heads. Take the tail meat out of the shells in a single piece, and cut it diagonally into medallions. Reserve the lobster shells for presentation.
To make the sauce: Combine the white wine, shallot, crushed peppercorns and star anise in a pan, bring to the boil and reduce by three-quarters. Add the fish stock and reduce again to a syrupy consistency. Add 300ml/10fl oz/1¼ cups of the cream, and reduce until slightly thickened. Pass the sauce through a fine sieve into a clean pan. Whip the remaining cream.
Put the lobster medallions into the sauce and heat gently for about 1 minute (Scottish lobster gets tough if you cook it for too long).

To serve: Heat the grill (broiler). Put the lobster medallions and claw meat back into the reserved shells. Add the mustard, parsley, whipped cream and hollandaise, to the sauce and season with salt and pepper. Cover the lobster with a little of the sauce and glaze under the hot grill. Serve with wild rice.

WILD RICE MIX

I never use wild rice on its own, but always mix it with pilaff rice and herbs to create a nice mix of flavours and textures.

SERVES 4

1 tbsp finely chopped onion
50ml/2fl oz/¼ cup oil
200g/7oz/scant cup long-grain white rice
500ml/18fl oz/2 cups boiling Vegetable Stock
  (see page 182) or water
1 bay leaf
50g/2oz/¼ cup wild rice
2 tbsp chopped mixed fresh herbs
salt and freshly ground pepper

To make the pilaff rice: Heat the oven to 180°C/350°F/Gas Mark 4. In a pan, sweat the onion in the oil until transparent. Add the white rice and stir until it is completely coated with oil. Add the boiling vegetable stock or water and the bay leaf, and season with salt and pepper. Cover and cook in the oven for about 20 minutes until tender.
Boil the wild rice in plenty of salted water for about 30 minutes until al dente . Drain and mix with the pilaff rice and herbs.

Seared Blue-fin Tuna on Crispy Vegetables and Beansprouts

You might think that this dish is not typical of The Savoy, and you would be right, yet it became popular years ago in the banqueting department. It is a very pleasant, light dinner dish that always goes down well with customers, and the cooking time is very short, which is a bonus.

SERVES 4

250g/9oz dried egg noodles
100g/3½oz/mangetouts (snow peas), trimmed and
  cut into lengths
4 x 150g/5oz blue fin tuna steaks
1 tbsp sesame oil
2 tbsp vegetable oil
5 spring onions (scallions), trimmed and sliced
5cm/2in fresh root ginger, peeled and chopped
100g/3½oz/scant 2 cups beansprouts
2 tbsp coriander (cilantro) leaves, shredded
2 tbsp soy sauce
1 tsp sesame seeds, toasted
3 limes, halved
salt and freshly ground pepper

Heat the oven to 200°C/400°F/Gas Mark 6. Bring a large pan of salted water to the boil. Add the egg noodles and mangetouts (snow peas), bring back to the boil, then turn off the heat, leave to stand for 5 minutes, and drain.
While the noodles are standing, season the tuna steaks. Heat a little sesame oil in a frying pan (skillet) and sear the tuna on both sides. Transfer it to an ovenproof dish and bake in the oven for 3 minutes until rare (tuna should be cooked like beef; ask your guests how they prefer theirs done).
Meanwhile, heat the vegetable oil in a frying pan (skillet), put the spring onions (scallions) and ginger, and cook for 2 minutes, then add the beansprouts and cook for another minute. Add the shredded coriander (cilantro) at the last moment.
Toss the cooked noodles in the soy sauce, the remaining sesame oil and the sesame seeds. Divide them among 4 plates. Squeeze some lime juice over the tuna steaks, arrange them on top of the noodles, and garnish with the spring onion and beansprout mixture.

Méli-Mélo of Lamb on Minted Pea Purée

Lamb is by far the most popular meat at The Savoy. This robust, flavoursome dish is a hybrid of a duck dish we used to serve some years ago. I substituted lamb for the duck confit in the potato cakes – and the rest is history. The potato cakes quickly became one of the most popular garnishes.

SERVES 4

4 x 50g/2oz lamb cutlets (chops)
4 x 50g/2oz fillet of lamb cut from the best end (neck slice), all skin removed
2 tbsp olive oil
2 garlic cloves, crushed
160g/5oz mixed vegetables (eg: carrots, green and yellow courgettes [zucchini], green beans, mouli [daikon]), cut into thick 10cm/4in long julienne and blanched
25g/1oz/2 tbsp butter
sea salt and freshly ground black pepper

FOR THE POTATO CAKE

400g/14oz potatoes (preferably Maris Piper), cut into 3 mm/⅛ in slices
2 tbsp oil
2 thyme sprigs, leaves only
120g/4oz Confit of Lamb (see recipe right)
200ml/7fl oz/scant 1 cup Chicken Stock (see page 180)

FOR THE PEA PURÉE

25g/1oz/2 tbsp chopped onion
2 tbsp oil
½ garlic clove, crushed
50ml/2fl oz/¼ cup dry white wine
5 tbsp double (heavy) cream
200g/7oz/1¾ cups frozen peas
½ tbsp shredded mint leaves

To make the potato cake: Heat the oven to 180°C/350°F/Gas Mark 4. Mix the potatoes with 1½ tbsp oil, add the thyme, and season with salt and pepper. In a round ovenproof dish, about 20cm/8in diameter, 4cm/1½in deep, make a 1cm/½in layer of sliced potatoes, then a 2cm/¾in layer of lamb confit, and top with a second 1cm/½in layer of potatoes. Boil the chicken stock to reduce it by half, and pour it over the potatoes.
Bake in the oven for 1½ hours, then remove and cool slightly. Place a plate on top as a weight. Chill for 4 hours, then cut into 4 wedges. Heat the rest of the oil in a non-stick pan, add the

wedges, and fry until lightly coloured on both sides. Replace in the oven for 10 minutes.
To make the pea purée: In a shallow pan, sweat the onion in half the oil until soft and translucent, add the garlic and sweat for another minute. Add the white wine and boil until reduced by two-thirds. Add the cream and reduce by half. Add the peas and heat through, season with salt and pepper, then blend coarsely with a hand-held blender. Stir in the mint at the last moment.
To cook the lamb: Reduce the oven temperature to 160°C/325°F/Gas Mark 3. Season all the pieces of lamb and seal in a little oil with crushed garlic. Place on a baking tray (cookie sheet) and cook in the oven, allowing 3 minutes for the cutlets (chops) and 5 minutes for the fillet. Allow to rest for 5 minutes.
To serve: Heat the mixed vegetable julienne in a little butter, and season. Spoon the minted pea purée into the middle of 4 plates, and place a wedge of potato cake beside it. Cut the lamb fillet into four pieces and arrange one piece with one cutlet on top of the pea purée. Top with the vegetable julienne, and serve.

CONFIT OF SHOULDER OF LAMB

Originally developed in Gascony, confits were used to tenderize tough and fatty pieces of duck legs and, more importantly, to preserve them. Nowadays, confits are made with all kinds of meat, but the basic principles remain the same. You can buy cans of goose fat in good delicatessens and supermarkets.

MAKES ABOUT 1KG/2¼LB

800g/1¾lb boned shoulder of lamb
3 garlic cloves, crushed
5 thyme sprigs, leaves only
500g/1lb 2 oz goose fat
sea salt and freshly ground black pepper

Heat the oven to 80°C/175°F or the lowest gas setting. Rub the lamb with sea salt and season with pepper. Rub with the crushed garlic and sprinkle with thyme. Cover and chill for 12 hours to help to draw out excess moisture from the meat. Pat it off before cooking. In a flameproof casserole, heat the goose fat to 80°C/175°F and put in the lamb, making sure it is completely submerged in the fat. Cover and cook in the oven for about 4 hours. Leave to cool. The confit is now ready to use, but you can leave it in the fat and chill it. It will keep for several weeks. Once you have used the lamb, keep the goose fat for cooking other warming dishes such as *cassoulet toulousienne* and *choucroûte*.

Lentil and Wild Mushroom Salad with Cumin-Scented Yogurt and Armenian Bread

For an interesting and colourful variation, you could make this substantial vegetarian salad with roasted red (bell) peppers instead of wild mushrooms. I love the contrasting texture of the Armenian bread, which is now always served in the restaurants instead of the classic Melba toast. It is wafer-thin and you can put on any topping you desire. I particularly like shallot rings, poppy seeds, any dried herbs, and paprika. It's also nice to make it in various shapes, as each one introduces a different texture.

SERVES 4

2 tbsp olive oil
½ onion, finely chopped
2 garlic cloves, crushed
120g/4oz/½ cup Puy lentils, soaked for 2 hours in 2 changes of water
200ml/7fl oz/scant 1 cup Vegetable Stock (see page 182)
1 shallot, finely chopped
120g/4oz mixed wild mushrooms (eg: girolles, chanterelles, ceps, black trumpets), trimmed, halved and blanched
2 tbsp shredded flat leaf parsley
50g/2oz/scant ½ cup broad (fava) beans, blanched and skinned
2 tomatoes, peeled, de-seeded and cut into strips
4 tbsp natural (plain) yogurt
pinch of ground cumin
2 tbsp shredded mint
8 pieces of Armenian Bread (see recipe right) or toasted pitta breads, to serve

FOR THE PUMPKIN SEED DRESSING

2 tbsp white wine vinegar
4 tbsp olive oil
4 tbsp pumpkin seed oil
salt and freshly ground pepper

To cook the lentils: Heat half the olive oil in a pan, add the onion, and sweat until soft and translucent. Add ½ of the garlic and sweat for another minute. Drain the lentils and add them to the pan together with the vegetable stock. Simmer until the lentils are tender and most of the stock has evaporated, then leave to cool. Make the pumpkin seed dressing by mixing all the ingredients. Add a little to the lentils and season with salt and pepper.
To cook the mushrooms: Sweat the shallot in the rest of the olive oil until translucent. Add the remaining garlic and sweat for another minute, then add the mushrooms and sweat for 1 more minute.

Season with salt and pepper and add the shredded parsley. Add the broad (fava) beans, tomatoes and remaining pumpkin seed dressing at the last moment. If you like, keep a few beans for garnish.
To serve: Place a spoonful of lentils on each plate and top with the mushrooms. Mix the yogurt, cumin and remaining garlic with the mint and place a spoonful of yogurt mix on top of the lentils, or serve it separately. Serve the salad with the Armenian bread.

ARMENIAN BREAD

FOR THE DOUGH

500g/1lb 2oz/4½ cups strong bread flour (T55 is best)
15g/½oz/1 tbsp garlic salt
250ml/9fl oz/generous 1 cup water
150ml/5fl oz/scant ⅔ cup olive oil

FOR THE TOPPING

100ml/3½fl oz/scant ½ cup water
100ml/3½fl oz/scant ½ cup olive oil
2 tsp garlic powder
½ onion, thinly sliced
1 tsp sesame seeds

To make the dough: Sift the flour and garlic salt into the bowl of an electric mixer fitted with the dough hook. Add the water and olive oil and work together for about 10 minutes to make an elastic dough. Divide the dough into 2 pieces and leave to rest for 20 minutes.
Heat the oven to 220°/425°F/Gas Mark 7. Grease a baking tray (cookie sheet) and stand it on an upturned mixing bowl so that the tray is about 10cm/4in above the work surface (counter).
Using your fingertips only, start to stretch out the dough to cover the tray, as if you were making strudel pastry. Be careful not to split it. Keep stretching the dough until it is paper-thin and overhanging the sides of the tray.
Mix the water with the olive oil and garlic powder and brush the mixture generously over the dough to make sure that it never dries out. Cut the dough into squares or triangles and sprinkle with the sliced onion and sesame seeds. Bake in the hot oven for 8 minutes. Leave the bread to cool and store it in an airtight container until needed. It will keep for up to 4 days.
To make poppy seed bread, just substitute 2 tbsp poppy seeds for the onion and sesame seeds.

Ginger Crème Brûlée with Sesame Tuiles

Very often it is the simple things that leave a lasting impression, and this crème brûlée with a twist is one of these stunningly simple things.

SERVES 4

75g/3oz fresh root ginger, peeled and very finely chopped
500ml/18fl oz/2¼ cups whipping (heavy) cream
6 egg yolks
100g/3½oz/½ cup caster (superfine) sugar
100g/3½oz/scant ½ cup brown sugar

FOR THE SESAME TUILES

25g/1oz/¼ cup icing (confectioners') sugar
25g/1oz/¼ cup plain (all-purpose) flour
25g/1oz/2 tbsp sesame seeds
25g/1oz/2 tbsp butter, melted
1½ tbsp orange juice, at room temperature
zest of ½ unwaxed orange, finely grated
butter, for greasing

Start by making the ginger cream at least 2 hours in advance: Combine the chopped ginger and cream in a pan and bring to the boil. Take the pan off the heat and leave to cool.
Whisk the egg yolks and caster (superfine) sugar until thoroughly mixed, then whisk in the cooled cream to make a custard. Stir, cover and chill for at least 2 hours to let the custard infuse (steep) with the ginger. Strain.
To cook the ginger creams: Heat the oven to 120°C/250°F/Gas Mark ½. Line a roasting tin (pan) with greaseproof (waxed) paper. Pour the custard into 4 small ramekins and stand them in the tin. Pour warm water into the tin, and cook in the oven for 40 minutes.
To glaze: Heat the grill (broiler) until very hot. Cool the ginger creams to room temperature, then sprinkle with a generous dusting of brown sugar, and glaze them under the grill until the sugar has turned deep brown.
To make the sesame tuiles: Mix together the sugar, flour and sesame seeds, then add the melted butter followed by the orange juice and grated zest. Place in the refrigerator and leave to rest for 1 hour. Meanwhile, heat the oven to 180°C/350°F/Gas Mark 4. Spread the mixture thinly over a buttered baking tray (cookie sheet) and bake in the oven for 8–10 minutes. Use a 7cm/2¾in round pastry (cookie) cutter to make 4 round tuiles. Remove and immediately drape the tuiles over a rolling pin to bend them into the traditional curved shape, or cut them into whatever shapes you like. Garnish each ginger brûlée with a sesame tuile, and serve immediately.

Frangipane Tartlets with Warm Balsamic-marinated Strawberries and Frozen Lemon Curd

These delicious light tartlets are simple to make and are a real treat. They can be served just as they are, or you could pipe a lattice of strawberry coulis and crème anglaise on the plates before putting on the tartlets, and top the lemon curd with a tiny sprig of mint – the choice is yours. The balsamic marinade will transform even flavourless glasshouse-grown strawberries into a delight.

SERVES 4

400g/14oz Sweet Shortcrust Pastry (see Passion Fruit Tart, page 66)

FOR THE FRANGIPANE

120g/4oz/½ cup unsalted (sweet) butter, softened
120g/4oz/1 cup icing (confectioners') sugar
120g/4oz eggs (about 3 large [extra large] eggs), beaten
25g/1oz/¼ cup plain (all-purpose) flour
120g/4oz/1 cup ground almonds
4 tsp dark rum
2 tbsp strawberry jam (jelly)

FOR THE WARM BALSAMIC-MARINATED STRAWBERRIES

400g/14oz/3½ cups strawberries hulled, washed and dried
70g/2½oz/⅓ cup caster (superfine) sugar
5 tbsp balsamic vinegar

To make the pastry cases (pie shells): Roll out the pastry to a thickness of about 3mm/⅛in. Cut out 4 rounds with a 12cm/4in pastry (cookie) cutter and use them to line four 10 cm/4 in tartlet tins (muffin pans). Place on a baking (cookie) sheet and chill for 20 minutes.
To make the frangipane: Cream the softened butter with the icing (confectioners') sugar, then gradually beat in the eggs. Sift the flour and ground almonds, and stir them into the butter mixture until smooth, then stir in the rum.
To bake the tartlets: Heat the oven to 160°C/325°F/Gas Mark 3. Remove the pastry cases from the refrigerator and brush them with strawberry jam (jelly). Spread on a 5mm/¼in layer of frangipane, and bake the tartlets in the oven for about 40 minutes until golden.
To cook the warm balsamic-marinated strawberries: Mix the sugar and balsamic vinegar and bring to the boil. Add the strawberries and warm them gently. Remove them from the marinade with a slotted spoon and place on the tartlets. Arrange a ball of frozen lemon curd on top.

Savoy Crêpes Suzette

These classic wafer-thin pancakes are traditionally made at the guest's table. The chef lights the Grand Marnier at the last moment, which always attracts glances from other diners.

SERVES 4

100g/3½oz/scant 1 cup plain (all-purpose) flour
pinch of salt
2 eggs
8 tbsp caster (superfine) sugar
300ml/10fl oz/1¼ cups milk
40g/1½oz/3 tbsp unsalted (sweet) butter
300ml/10fl oz/1¼ cups freshly squeezed orange juice
zest of 2 oranges
2 star anise
2 vanilla pods (beans), split lengthways
50ml/2fl oz/scant ¼ cup Grand Marnier
juice of ½ lemon
250g/9oz Vanilla Ice Cream, to serve (see page 188)

To make the crêpe batter: Sift the flour and salt into a large bowl, then add the eggs, half the sugar, and about a quarter of the milk. Mix to a thick batter, then gradually stir in the rest of the milk. If there are any lumps, pass the batter through a fine sieve.
Melt the butter in a pan until it begins to froth and whisk half into the batter.

To cook the crêpes: Heat a 20cm/8in non-stick frying pan (skillet). Brush the inside with a little of the remaining butter, and ladle in enough batter to cover the base of the pan in a thin layer, tilting the pan gently to spread it evenly. Cook for 30 seconds, turn the crêpe over, and cook for another 30 seconds. The crêpe should be evenly browned on both sides. Take it out of the pan, and continue to make 7 more crêpes in the same way.

To make the sauce: Heat the remaining sugar in a wide pan, stirring constantly until amber coloured. Add the orange juice, zest and star anise, and scrape in the seeds from the vanilla pods (beans), Simmer the sauce until reduced by half.

To serve: Heat 4 plates. Take a crêpe, lay it in the sauce, then turn it and fold it in half, then into half again. Arrange all the crêpes like this in the pan, squeeze on a little lemon juice, and add the Grand Marnier. Leave to infuse (steep) for 1 minute, then serve 2 crêpes on each plate. At the last moment, top with the vanilla ice cream, which will melt deliciously over the hot crêpes.

Soufflé Rothschild

This classic Savoy dish was introduced by Escoffier just before the turn of the nineteenth century. Over a hundred years later, it still features on the dinner menu, so you can truly say that here is a dish which has stood the test of time! The only difference is that the soufflé is now accompanied by burnt orange ice cream, whereas Escoffier would have served it with floppy whipped cream. The candied fruit adds a delightful, unusual texture, and introduces great flavours.

SERVES 4

120g/4oz/½ cup butter, melted
130g /4½oz/⅔ cup caster (superfine) sugar
500ml/18fl oz/2¼ cups milk
70g/2½oz/generous ½ cup flour
10 egg yolks
1 tbsp candied orange peel, chopped
1 tbsp glacé (candied) cherries, chopped
1 tbsp candied angelica, chopped
8 egg whites
1 tsp cornflour (cornstarch)
250g/9oz Burnt Orange Ice Cream (see page 189)

To prepare the soufflé dishes: Heat the oven to 220°C/425°F/Gas Mark 7. Brush the insides of 4 individual soufflé dishes with melted butter. It is essential to make sure that the entire surface is well covered. Pour the sugar into a dish and rotate to cover the surface. Tip the excess into the next dish, and repeat to coat all the dishes.
To make the soufflé mixture: In a pan, bring the milk to the boil. Mix 80g/3oz/6 tbsp of the butter with the flour and stir it into the boiling milk.
Mix the egg yolks with 100g/3½oz/scant ¼ cup of the sugar. Stir in a little of the hot milk mixture, then stir this back into the boiling milk. Bring to the boil again, stirring constantly, then take off the heat. Add the candied peel, cherries and angelica, and cool to room temperature.
In a large, very clean bowl, whisk the egg whites to stiff peaks, then add the cornflour (cornstarch) and any remaining sugar. Fold a quarter of this mixture into the soufflé mix to soften it. Gently fold in the remaining egg whites, then fill the soufflé dishes to the top. Bake the soufflés in the oven for about 25 minutes until well risen.
To serve: Scoop the ice cream into quenelles and place 1 in each spoon. Place the soufflé dishes on serving plates, and serve with a spoon of ice cream on the side.

Cherry Tart with Cinnamon Ice Cream

This is an adaptation of my mother's recipe. We used to make it together with home-grown cherries. I always remember eating it still warm from the oven when I was a child. What a happy memory! The excellent raspberry sauce which accompanies the tart can be served with many other desserts, including Savoy Summer Pudding (see page 64). Serve it as a deliciously healthy alternative to cream.

SERVES 4–6

225g/8oz/2 cups plain (all-purpose) flour
1 tsp baking powder
½ tsp salt
120g/4oz/½ cup unsalted (sweet) butter, chilled
100g/3½oz/½ cup caster (superfine) sugar
finely grated zest of 1 unwaxed lemon
1 egg
500g/1lb 2oz fresh cherries, washed, dried and stoned
a little egg white
200ml/7fl oz/scant 1 cup natural (plain) yogurt
shavings of a cinnamon stick, to decorate

FOR SERVING

Raspberry Sauce (see page 185)
250g/9oz Cinnamon Ice Cream (see page 189)

To make the pastry case (pie shell): Combine the flour, baking powder and salt in a bowl. Cut the butter into cubes and rub into the flour until the mixture resembles coarse breadcrumbs. Add all but 1 tbsp sugar, the lemon zest and egg, and mix together to form a dough.
Wrap and chill in the refrigerator for 1 hour.
Grease a 15cm/6in diameter flan ring and place it on a baking (cookie)sheet, or use a loose-based flan tin (quiche pan). Roll out two-thirds of the dough to a 5mm/¼in thickness and use it to line the flan ring or tin. Pack the cherries tightly in the flan case and press them firmly into the dough.
Roll out the remaining dough into a round 5mm/¼in thick. Lay it over the cherries, cut off the excess dough, then press the edges gently down inside the ring to seal. Chill in the refrigerator for 20 minutes.

To bake the tart: Heat the oven to 190°C/375°F/Gas Mark 5. Brush the top of the tart with egg white and sprinkle with the reserved sugar. Bake the tart for 25–30 minutes, until the pastry is golden brown. Leave it to cool slightly, then remove the flan ring or the side of tin. Cut the tart into neat wedges.
To serve: Make a small pool of raspberry sauce on each plate and add a drop of yogurt in the middle. If you wish, feather the two together, using a wooden cocktail stick (toothpick) or skewer. Place a piece of tart on the edge of the sauce.
To shape the ice cream: Dip a dessert spoon in hot water, then scrape it across the surface of the ice cream, rolling it into the spoon to make a neat quenelle shape. Place a quenelle of ice cream beside the tart. Decorate the ice cream with shavings of cinnamon, and serve.

Chocolate Trifle

Trifle has always had its place in the English dessert repertoire, and when the time came to put away the old-fashioned sweet trolleys, the chefs had to think about retaining a much-loved favourite of Savoy customers, but in a different form. This is the latest reincarnation. As always, these matters are under constant review, and things could change tomorrow.

SERVES 4

FOR THE SYRUP

150g/5oz/¾ cup caster (superfine) sugar
300ml/10fl oz/1¼ cups water
4 tsp lemon juice
3 gelatine leaves
50ml/2fl oz/¼ cup Grand Marnier

FOR THE CHOCOLATE CUSTARD
½ vanilla pod (bean)
250ml/9fl oz/generous 1 cup milk
1 egg yolk
2 tbsp sugar
150g/5oz couverture or plain (bittersweet) cooking chocolate

4 gelatine leaves4 tbsp whipping (heavy) cream, very lightly whipped
20 large orange segments, seeds and membrane removed
120g/4oz Sponge Cake, (see page 169)
1 tbsp crème de cacao liqueur
8 lychees, peeled and stoned (pitted)
200 ml/7fl oz/scant 1 cup Orange Sauce (see recipe below), to serve

First make the syrup: Put the sugar and water in a small pan and dissolve the sugar over a medium heat. Add the lemon juice and bring to the boil. Soak the gelatine leaves in water, squeeze them, then stir into the hot syrup and leave to cool. Strain and stir in the Grand Marnier.

To make the chocolate custard: Split the vanilla pod (bean) lengthways, scrape out the seeds, add them to the milk, and bring to the boil. In a bowl, whisk the egg yolk with the sugar, then pour on the boiling milk, whisking constantly. Return the mixture to the pan and bring it back to boiling point, stirring all the time until the custard coats the back of a spoon. Take the pan off the heat, add the chocolate, and stir until it has melted.

Soak the gelatine in water, squeeze it dry and stir it into the custard. Cool to blood temperature, then fold in the whipped cream.

To assemble the trifles: Pour 5mm/¼in of the syrup into 4 dome-shaped moulds or individual white ramekins, and chill until set. Put 2 orange segments on top, pour on another 5mm/¼in syrup, and replace in the refrigerator to set again.

Pour in a 5mm/¼in layer of chocolate custard. Break the sponge cake into small pieces, soak them in the crème de cacao, and divide them between the moulds or ramekins. Pour on a 1cm/½in layer of chocolate custard and chill until set.

Top the trifles with the remaining orange segments and cover with the remaining syrup. Chill for about 2 hours until set.

To serve: Warm the blade of a thin knife, run it around the edge of the trifles, and turn them out on to serving plates. Cut the lychees into small pieces, mix them into the orange sauce, and pour a little around the trifles.

ORANGE SAUCE

3 vanilla pods (beans), split and scraped
500ml/18fl oz/2¼ cups fresh orange juice
zest of 4 oranges
50ml/2fl oz/¼ cup Grand Marnier

Put the vanilla pods (beans), orange juice and zest in a pan, bring to the boil and boil until reduced to 200ml/7fl oz/scant 1cup. Stir in the Grand Marnier.

Fantasy of Apples with Sticky Calvados Sauce

For me, apples are among the most exciting produce; there are a hundred and one ways of preparing them – all great to eat and usually very refreshing. A good apple is one of the cheapest and most undervalued ingredients in the kitchen, yet it can bring so much joy. This recipe combines apples cooked in four different ways. It is very important to choose the right apple to suit the recipe, as each variety has its own particular character. Some don't cook well, while others may be too sweet or too tart. For the sorbet (sherbet), I suggest using Bramleys; for the tart either Granny Smith or Spartan; and for the baking apple, I would again use a Granny Smith or Cox's orange pippin in season.

SERVES 4

FOR THE BAKED APPLES

25g/1oz/scant ¼ cup sultanas (golden raisins), soaked in Calvados
40g/2oz/¼ cup soft brown sugar
4 Granny Smith apples, cored and scored around the circumference

FOR THE APPLE TARTS

200g/7oz Puff Pastry (see page 186)
100g/3½oz Frangipane (see page 187)
4 Spartan apples, peeled, cored, halved, then cut
  into 3mm/⅛in slices
20g/¾oz/scant ¼ cup icing (confectioners') sugar

FOR THE SORBET (SHERBET)

200g/7oz/scant 1 cup apple purée
20g/¾oz liquid glucose
200ml/7fl oz/scant 1 cup Stock Syrup (see page 185)
juice of 1 lemon

FOR THE SAUCE

50g/2oz/¼ cup caster (superfine) sugar
50ml/2fl oz/¼ cup water
10g/¼oz liquid glucose
50g/2oz/¼ cup unsalted (sweet) butter
150ml/5fl oz/⅔ cup double (heavy) cream
3 tbsp Calvados

TO DECORATE

apple mint sprigs
2 tbsp chopped mixed pistachios and walnuts

For the baked apples: Heat the oven to 180°C/350°F/Gas Mark 4. Mix the soaked sultanas (golden raisins) with the brown sugar and stuff into the cored Granny Smiths. Bake in the oven for about 40–50 minutes until soft. (Test by inserting a small knife.)
For the apple tarts: Increase the oven temperature to 200°C/400°F/Gas mark 6. Roll out the puff pastry into a square about 3mm/⅛in thick, then cut it into 5 x 8cm/2 x 3¼in rectangles. Prick these with a fork, then smear a thin layer of frangipane over the pastry, and top it very carefully with the sliced apples. Chill the tarts for 20 minutes, then bake in the oven for 20–25 minutes. Dust with icing (confectioners') sugar and glaze with a blowtorch or under a hot grill (broiler).
To make the apple sorbet (sherbet): Mix the apple purée, glucose, stock syrup and lemon juice, and churn in an ice cream maker until frozen.
For the sauce: Cook the sugar and water with the glucose until pale amber, then stir in the butter and cream. Finally, add the calvados.
To serve: Place a baked apple and an apple tart on each plate. Using 2 spoons, shape a quenelle of sorbet, put it beside the tart and garnish with a sprig of apple mint. Pour a little sauce around the baked apple and sprinkle with the pistachios and walnuts.

Cheese Petits Fours

This is a refreshingly different way to serve cheese. I sometimes like to end a meal on a savoury note instead of with the usual sweet petits fours – just right for finishing off a little port or red wine. The five ideas I have given here are only suggestions; you can use any kind of cheese on any kind of bread. Use your imagination.

TARTLET CASES (SHELLS)

MAKES ABOUT 16

100g/3½oz/scant ½ cup unsalted (sweet) butter
225g/8oz/2 cups plain (all-purpose) flour, sifted with pinch of salt
8 tsp cold water

Rub the butter into the flour and salt, and mix to a firm dough with the water. Leave to rest in a cool place for 20 minutes, then roll out as thinly as possible and use to line miniature muffin tins (pans). Place empty muffin tins on top to weigh the dough down.
Heat the oven to 200°C/400°F/Gas Mark 6. Bake blind (without filling) for 10 minutes. Remove the top muffin tins and bake for a further 5 minutes. Remove them from the tins and leave to cool.

BRIE TARTLETS

MAKES 4

4 Tartlet Cases (shells) (see recipe above)
½ tsp cranberry sauce
dill sprigs
poppy seeds
sesame seeds

FOR THE FILLING

25g/1oz Brie cheese, rind removed
1 small (medium) egg yolk
pinch of nutmeg
2 tbsp single (light) cream
salt and freshly ground pepper

Combine all the ingredients for the filling in a food processor and work until smooth.
Heat the grill (broiler). Fill the tartlet cases (shells) with the cheese filling and place under the hot grill until golden. Top each tartlet with a little cranberry sauce and garnish with a frond of dill. Place the tartlets attractively on a plate and sprinkle with a few poppy and sesame seeds.

GOAT'S CHEESE CROSTINI

MAKES 4

½ small goat's cheese (eg: crottin de chavignol, marinated in herb olive oil (see Tomato Tarts, page   )
1 egg, beaten
½ tbsp poppy seeds
½ tbsp sesame seeds
2 tbsp olive oil
4 crostini or small rounds of toasted bread
butter, for spreading
treviso lettuce leaves

Cut the goat's cheese into 4 pieces and dip them in beaten egg, then turn in the mixed poppy and sesame seeds until lightly coated. Heat the olive oil in a non-stick frying pan (skillet), put in the cheese, and fry until the sesame seeds are golden brown. Spread the crostini with butter, and place a couple of Treviso leaves on each. Arrange the warm goat's cheese on top, and serve.

COTTAGE CHEESE TARTLETS

MAKES 4

1 spring onion (scallion), trimmed
4 small mint sprigs
40g/1½oz/scant ¼ cup cottage cheese
4 Tartlet Cases (shells) (see recipe left)
salt and freshly ground pepper

Cut the spring onion (scallion) into thin slices and chop with half the mint. Put the cottage cheese in a bowl and mix with the spring onion (scallion) and mint. Season with salt and pepper, and fill the tartlet cases (shells) with this mixture. Garnish each one with a tiny sprig of mint.

BEAUFORT WITH ARTICHOKE HEARTS

MAKES 4

40g/1½oz Beaufort cheese
2 artichoke hearts, cooked and marinated
¼ tsp English (hot) mustard
chervil sprig

Heat the grill (broiler). Cut the Beaufort into 4 pieces and halve the artichokes. Place a piece of cheese on each one and melt lightly under the grill. Top with a little mustard and a chervil leaf.

BRIOCHE CROÛTE WITH MANGO CHUTNEY AND ROQUEFORT

MAKES 4

2 slices of Brioche (see page 27)
unsalted (sweet) butter, for spreading
5 tsp mango chutney
50g/2oz Roquefort cheese
4 pine nuts

Using a pastry (cookie) cutter, stamp out 4 neat rounds from the brioche slices and toast lightly on both sides. Spread butter and mango chutney on top. Crumble the Roquefort, sprinkle it over the chutney, and garnish each croûte with a pine nut.

Supper and Light Meals

A hundred years ago, late-night dining out in England was an impossibility. The licensing laws decreed that restaurants must close at 11pm, and The Savoy was no exception – highly inconvenient for the sybaritic Prince of Wales (later Edward V11), who loved to enjoy a post-theatre supper with Lily Langtry and other thespian companions. What the Prince of Wales wants, he usually gets. The licensing laws were duly changed; restaurants could remain open until after midnight, and The Savoy Restaurant was among the first to offer late-night suppers – a tradition that the hotel is proud to continue today.

Evening dining at The Savoy is not all grandeur and formality. Guests can come hotfoot from the Savoy Theatre or other nearby theatres to enjoy a relaxed supper or a casual light bite. In the kitchens, the dinner brigade goes home at 10.30pm, but the night chefs have arrived to take their place, ready to prepare supper, room service and snacks for hungry guests. The Savoy kitchens never sleep!

The Upstairs Restaurant is noted for its Asian food, light and digestible late at night. At the counter, Japanese chefs prepare the freshest sushi and sashimi, crispy spring rolls and delicate curries. If your preference is for traditional supper dishes – Devon fish pie or crab, fishcakes and risotto, the kitchens will provide them, alongside beef with *marchand de vin* sauce or lamb cutlets. Sometimes a snack is all that's required; then the chefs will gladly rustle up a pitta bread pizza or special club sandwich.

Most guests who come for supper prefer to eat lightly, but they like to drink expensively. Buoyed up by the show they have just seen, they tend to be on a high and bubbling with enthusiasm, so Champagne is often the order of the day (or night).

Their enthusiasm is infectious; supper at The Savoy is always a celebration.

Gazpacho with Seared Scallops and Sugar Snaps

There are many different recipes for gazpacho and all are delicious on a hot summer's day. As always, however, the chefs are constantly seeking to intensify the flavours in their recipes and I think they have succeeded brilliantly with this dish, which is gutsy and honest, and full of intense summer flavours. The hot scallops topped with caviar offer an interesting contrast to the chilled soup.

SERVES 4

600g/1¼ lb tomatoes, cut into quarters
300g/11oz cucumber, cut into quarters
50g/2oz red (bell) pepper, de-seeded and cut into large cubes
50g/2oz green (bell) pepper, de-seeded and cut into large cubes
100g/3½oz/scant ½ cup chopped onion
½ garlic clove, crushed
25g/1oz/½ cup fresh white breadcrumbs
2 tbsp olive oil
3 tbsp water
3 tbsp red wine vinegar
1 tsp tomato ketchup
pinch of oregano
1 tsp Mayonnaise (see page 183)
salt and freshly ground black pepper

FOR THE GARNISH

10 sugar snaps or mangetouts (snow peas)
4 scallops
1 tsp olive oil
juice of ½ lemon
20g/¾oz/1½ tbsp oscietra caviar
4 gold leaves, to garnish

To make the chilled gazpacho: Mix the tomatoes, cucumber, (bell) peppers, onion, garlic, breadcrumbs, olive oil, water, red wine vinegar, ketchup and oregano. Season with salt and pepper, cover and marinate for at least 24 hours in the refrigerator, stirring occasionally.

Process the marinated soup ingredients in a blender or food processor, stir in the mayonnaise, adjust the seasoning, and pass the gazpacho through a fine sieve.

To prepare the garnish: Fill a pan with plenty of salted water, bring to the boil, and plunge in the sugar snaps or mangetouts (snow peas) for a few seconds. Drain and refresh in iced water. Drain again and cut into small dice.

Season the scallops and sear them briefly in the olive oil until coloured and barely cooked. Add the lemon juice and reduce it, turning the scallops in the juice. Remove them from the pan.

To serve: Pour the gazpacho into chilled deep plates, arrange a heap of diced sugar snaps in the middle, and top with a scallop and a spoonful of caviar. Place a gold leaf on top of the caviar.

Baked Figs with Goat's Cheese and Coriander (Cilantro) Salad

This is a very delicate appetizer and the ingredients look somewhat low-key. But these figs pack a surprising punch and are full of character – perfect to begin a light supper.

SERVES 4

FOR THE GOAT'S CHEESE FILLING
2 small goat's cheeses (eg: crottin de chavignol)
a rosemary sprig
300ml/10fl oz/1¼ cups olive oil
100ml/3½fl oz/scant ½ cup double (heavy) cream
6 black figs
finely grated zest of ½ orange
sea salt

FOR THE CORIANDER (CILANTRO) SALAD
2 carrots, peeled
2 spring onions (scallions)
4 radishes
25g/1oz/½ cup coriander (cilantro) leaves
50g/2oz/1 cup wild rocket (arugula)
juice of ½ lemon
50ml/2fl oz/¼ cup Beetroot Glaze (see recipe right),
   to garnish

To make the cheese filling: Put the cheeses and rosemary in the olive oil and leave for at least 3 hours or, better still, overnight. Take them out of the oil and pat dry with kitchen paper (paper towels). Crumble them into a bowl and stir in the cream. Reserve the rosemary and olive oil.
To cook the figs: Heat the oven to 200°C/400°F/Gas Mark 6. Cut the figs in half, sprinkle with a little sea salt and the orange zest, and top with the cheese filling. Place the rosemary on a baking tray (cookie sheet) and set the figs on the tray. Bake in the oven for 6–7 minutes until the cheese has melted and is lightly coloured. Meanwhile, make the coriander salad. Cut the carrots, spring onions (scallions) and radishes into very fine strips and mix them with the coriander (cilantro) leaves and rocket (arugula). It is essential that the rocket leaves are small and the julienne of carrots and radishes are very thin. Be sure to make the salad with equal quantities of every ingredient so that you can see each one.
To serve: Whisk the lemon juice with a little of the reserved olive oil and toss the salad in this dressing. Place 3 fig halves on each plate and top with the coriander salad. Pour the beetroot (beet) glaze over the figs.

BEETROOT (BEET) GLAZE

200ml/7fl oz/scant 1 cup beetroot (beet) juice
5 tbsp olive oil

Reduce the beetroot (beet) juice by four-fifths. Cool and whisk in the olive oil.

Crab Meat with Granny Smith Apple Jelly

The unexpected combination of tart Granny Smith jelly and the delicate white crab meat work wonderfully together in this very light and elegant appetizer, which is perfect for a spring or early summer supper.

SERVES 4

4 Granny Smith apples
3 tbsp Stock Syrup (see page 185)
4 tsp dry white wine
4 tsp lemon juice
2 gelatine leaves
juice of ½ lemon
8 mint leaves
165g/5½oz/⅔ cup white crab meat, flaked and all cartilage removed
2 tbsp crème fraîche
2 tbsp Mayonnaise (see page 183)

FOR THE SALAD GARNISH

100ml/3½fl oz/scant ½ cup olive oil
2 handfuls of frisée lettuce
1 handful of lamb's lettuce (corn salad)
salt and freshly ground pepper

To make the dried apple rounds: Heat the oven to 80°C/175°F/ or the lowest gas setting. Cut 12 paper-thin rounds of apple and lay them out on greaseproof (waxed) paper or a silicone mat. Mix the stock syrup with the white wine and half the lemon juice, brush the mixture over the apple slices, and dry out for 2 hours in the low oven or until they are very crisp.

To make the Granny Smith jelly: Juice the remaining apples in a juicer and place in a pan. Soak the gelatine in cold water. Gently heat the apple juice and add the soaked gelatine, stirring until it has dissolved completely. Chill until set.

To prepare the salad garnish: Mix the remaining lemon juice with the olive oil, season with salt and pepper and toss the frisée and lambs' lettuce (corn salad) in the dressing.

To serve: Mix the crab meat with the crème fraîche and mayonnaise. Shred the mint leaves, add them to the crab meat, and season with salt. Divide the crab meat among 4 plates, top with a dried apple round, then some dressed salad. Put on another apple round, then more crab meat, and salad, and finish with an apple round. Chop the Granny Smith jelly and arrange it around the edge.

Game Salad with Wild Mushrooms and Port-Glazed Shallots

This dish is always a bestseller at The Savoy throughout the game season. You can use any kind of game and play around endlessly, so this popular appetizer could change from day to day.

SERVES 4

165g/5½oz venison loin, all membrane removed
2 oven-ready partridges
1 oven-ready teal
165g/5½ oz wild mushrooms (eg: girolles, black trumpets,
  chanterelles, ceps)
350g/12oz shallots, peeled
125ml/4fl oz/½ cup olive oil
2 garlic cloves, crushed
15g/½oz/½ cup flat parsley leaves, washed and shredded
150ml/5fl oz/⅔ cup port
2 tbsp redcurrant jelly
salt and freshly ground pepper

To cook the game: Heat the oven to 200°C/400°F/Gas Mark 6.
Season the venison, partridge and teal, and lay the game birds in
a roasting tin (pan) resting on one leg. Add the venison and roast
in the oven until pink. The venison will need 8 minutes; the birds
will take a total of 12 minutes – 4 minutes on one leg, 4 minutes
on the other and a final 4 minutes on their backs. Remove from
the oven and leave to rest in a warm place for 10 minutes. Take
the birds off the bone, remove the thigh bones from the legs, and
keep warm.

To cook the wild mushrooms: Trim the mushrooms and cut them
in half if necessary, then blanch them briefly in boiling water and
drain. Finely chop 1 of the shallots and sweat it in 4 tsp of the olive
oil until soft and translucent, then add the garlic and sweat for
another minute. Add the mushrooms and heat gently, season with
salt and pepper and, at the last moment, add the shredded parsley.

To cook the port-glazed shallots: Blanch the remaining shallots for
2 minutes in fast-boiling salted water, drain and refresh. Heat the
remaining olive oil in a non-stick shallow pan and add the shallots
in a single layer; they should all be touching the pan and the base
of the must be completely covered. Turn the heat up high and
brown the shallots all over. Add the port and redcurrant jelly, turn
down the heat and cook until the liquid is reduced to a syrup and
the shallots are tender. Season lightly with salt and pepper.

To serve: Divide the shallots among the plates. Carve the
venison and the partridge and teal breasts into 5mm/¼in thick
slices. Arrange all the game on top of the shallots and sprinkle
on the wild mushrooms.

Poached Eggs on Smoked Haddock and Toasted English Muffins

This dish is an adaptation of the old dish called "Haddock Monte Carlo", which has featured on The Savoy menu since the very beginning – and I'm sure that it still will be around as long as food is served at The Savoy. A great lunch or supper appetizer.

SERVES 4

4 thin slices of pancetta
100ml/3½fl oz/scant ½ cup vinegar
4 organic eggs
100ml/3½fl oz/⅔ cup milk
200g/7oz smoked haddock fillets, skinned
200ml/7fl oz/scant 1 cup double (heavy) cream
1 leek, trimmed, washed and outside leaves removed
25g/1oz/2 tbsp butter
2 English muffins, cut in half
15 basil leaves
125ml/4fl oz/½ cup freshly-made Hollandaise Sauce (see page 183)
freshly ground pepper

FOR THE GARNISH, OPTIONAL

100ml/3½fl oz/scant ½ cup olive oil
juice of ½ lemon
275g/10oz mixed salad leaves (greens) (eg: frisée, rocket [arugula],
  oak leaf lettuce, radicchio),

To dry the pancetta: Heat the oven to 80°C/175°F or its lowest gas setting. Arrange the pancetta on a tray lined with greaseproof (waxed) paper, then lay an identical tray on top and press it down on the pancetta. Place in the oven for 3 hours until very dry. Leave to cool, and keep in an airtight container.

Pour 400ml/14fl oz/1¾ cups water and the vinegar into a deep pan, bring to the boil, then reduce to a simmer. Do not add salt, as it would destroy the protein in the egg white and spoil the shape of the poached egg.

To poach the eggs: Crack an egg into a cup, and slide it into the simmering water. Repeat with the other 3 eggs; you will probably be able to fit all 4 into the pan at once. If not, cook in two batches. Simmer the eggs for 3–4 minutes, until the whites have set around the yolks. Remove with a slotted spoon and cool in iced water.

To cook the haddock: Mix the milk with an equal quantity of water in a pan and bring to the boil. Add the smoked haddock and poach for about 4 minutes. Leave to cool, then drain and flake the fish.

Boil the cream to reduce it by half. Cut the leek lengthways into quarters, then into 5mm/¼in dice. Melt the butter in a heavy pan and stir in the leeks. Season with pepper, cover the pan and cook quickly for about 5 minutes, stirring frequently. Add the haddock and the reduced cream, and season with pepper. Keep warm. Toast the muffins. Shred the basil leaves and stir them into the warm hollandaise.

Whisk the olive oil and lemon juice with a little salt and pepper, and toss the salad leaves (greens) in this dressing.

To serve: Reheat the poached eggs in simmering salted water for approximately 3 minutes (they almost take as long to reheat as they do to cook). Lift them out with a slotted spoon, dry on a tea (dish) towel, and divide the haddock mixture among the toasted muffin halves. Top each half with a poached egg and pour a little of the hollandaise on top. Place a muffin on each plate, garnish with the salad leaves and top with a slice of dried pancetta.

Lemon Sole Salad
on Tarragon Cream Sauce

This lovely summer appetizer is deeply rooted in the classic Savoy style, but I have changed the presentation. What really makes the dish is the flavour of the tomato and tarragon sauce. Lemon sole is much cheaper than Dover sole, and works well in this cold dish, as it is less meaty than its expensive cousin.

SERVES 4

8 lemon sole fillets, skinned
250g/9oz fish mousse
1 shallot, finely chopped
1 star anise
2 tbsp tarragon leaves, stalks reserved
½ tsp black peppercorns, crushed
100ml/3½fl oz/scant ½ cup white wine
300ml/10fl oz/1¼ cups Fish Stock (see page 180)

FOR THE SAUCE

3 plum tomatoes, chopped
300ml/10fl oz/1¼ cups double (heavy) cream
salt and freshly ground black pepper

FOR THE GARNISH

1 small handful each of rocket (arugula) and frisée lettuce
3 tbsp Lemon Dressing (see page 182)

Heat the oven to 180°C/350°F/Gas Mark 4. Pat the lemon sole fillets dry with kitchen paper (paper towels) and season with salt and pepper. Spread a spoonful of fish mousse over half of each fillet and fold the other half over the mousse.

To cook the sole fillets: Butter an ovenproof dish and put in the filled fillets. Sprinkle with the shallot, star anise, reserved tarragon stalks and crushed peppercorns. Pour over the wine and stock, and cover with foil. Bake in the oven 8 minutes, then transfer the sole fillets to another dish, reserving the cooking juices separately. Cover the sole with cling film (plastic wrap) and leave to cool, but do not chill the fish as this would impair the flavour.

To make the sauce: Pour the reserved cooking juices into a pan, add the tomatoes and reduce to one-quarter. Add the cream and reduce by half, then season with salt and pepper and pass the sauce through a fine sieve, pressing the tomatoes hard to extract all the flavour and colour. Chop the tarragon leaves and add them to the sauce, and cool the sauce to room temperature.

To serve: Put 2 sole fillets on each plate and pour a little sauce over them. Toss the salad in the dressing and place a small mound on top of the fish.

Wild Mushroom and Tofu (Beancurd) Strudels on a Bed of Mediterranean Vegetables

Vegetarians and non-vegetarians enjoy this very unusual and tasty dish. I love it for its versatility; it can be made with almost any vegetables, is very quick to prepare, and is equally suitable for a main dish as well as an appetizer.

SERVES 4

FOR THE STRUDELS

1 onion, finely chopped

3 tbsp olive oil

2 garlic cloves, crushed

½ leek, outside leaves removed, cut into 5mm/¼in pieces, and washed

400g/14oz mixed wild mushrooms (eg: girolles, chanterelles, ceps, shiitake, black trumpets), trimmed and blanched

8 sheets of filo or brik pastry

1 egg, lightly beaten

200g/7oz tofu (beancurd)

oil, for deep-frying

salt and freshly ground pepper

FOR THE GARNISH

350g/12oz new potatoes, preferably Jersey royals

½ tsp ground cumin

40g/1½oz pickled ginger

350g/12oz Mediterranean Vegetables (see page 187)

25g/1oz/2 tbsp unsalted (sweet) butter

2 tbsp snipped chives

4 tbsp Basil Oil (see page 182)

First cook the potatoes: Scrub them well, then boil in salted water with the cumin until tender. Drain and keep hot.

To make the wild mushroom filling: Sweat the onion in the olive oil until soft and translucent, add the garlic and sweat for another minute. Add the leek and cook until soft, then add the mushrooms, sweat for another minute, and season with salt and pepper. Leave the mixture to cool.

To make the strudels: Lay a sheet of filo or brik on a table, brush it with the beaten egg, and top with a second sheet. Spoon a 2cm/¾in x 20cm/8in strip of mushroom mixture on to the pastry. Cut the tofu (beancurd) into 2cm/¾in strips and place them on top of the mushroom filling. Brush the pastry all over with beaten egg, then fold in the ends and roll the strudel into a cylinder. Make 3 more strudels in this way.

Heat the frying oil to 160C°/320°F in a deep-fat fryer. Put in the strudels, 1 at a time, and fry until golden brown. Drain on kitchen paper (paper towels). Keep the oil hot to fry the pickled ginger.

To serve: Heat the Mediterranean vegetables and divide them among the middle of 4 plates. Cut the strudel rolls at an angle into 3 cylinders of different heights, and arrange them beside the vegetables. Deep-fry the pickled ginger very quickly.

At the last moment, toss the potatoes in the butter and snipped chives. Drizzle the basil oil around the vegetables, arrange the potatoes around the edge, and sprinkle with the deep-fried ginger.

Langoustines in Their Pyjamas
with Mango Sauce

Because this dish frequently appears on the supper menu, I imagined that the filo pastry wrapping for the langoustines might be their nightwear – hence the delightful if somewhat whimsical name. The crispness of the pastry contrasts well with the delicate texture of the crustaceans. Tiger prawns (jumbo shrimp) can be substituted for the langoustines.

SERVES 4

20 raw langoustines or tiger prawns (jumbo shrimp) in their shells
20 x 12cm/5in squares of filo pastry
50g/2oz/¼ cup unsalted (sweet) butter, melted
1 egg yolk, lightly beaten
vegetable oil, for frying
sea salt and freshly ground pepper

FOR THE MANGO SAUCE

1 large ripe mango
1 hard-boiled (hard-cooked) egg yolk
4 tbsp Mayonnaise (see page 183)
2 tsp finely shredded basil leaves

First make the mango sauce: Peel the mango and cut off the flesh from the flat central stone (pit); you should have about 100g/3½oz/1 cup flesh. Chop it coarsely, place in a food processor or blender with the hard-boiled (hard-cooked) egg yolk and mayonnaise, and whizz until smooth. Stir in the shredded basil, and season to taste with salt and pepper. Set the sauce aside.
Peel the langoustines or prawns (shrimp), then make a shallow incision down their rounded backs, and remove the dark intestinal vein. Rinse the langoustines or prawns and pat dry with kitchen paper (paper towels). Season with sea salt and pepper.
To dress the langoustines in their pyjamas: Lay a filo square on the work surface (counter) and brush it with melted butter. Set a basil leaf in the centre and put a langoustine or prawn on top. Lightly beat the egg yolk and brush a little on the edges of the filo square. Fold opposite sides of the square over the langoustine. Press the long side to seal, then press the ends together to seal them. Wrap and seal the rest of the langoustines or prawns in the same way.

To cook the langoustines: Heat the vegetable oil to 165–175°C/ 325–350°F in a deep-fat fryer. When the oil is hot, add the langoustines in their pyjamas, 4 at a time. Fry for 3 minutes or until golden and crisp, turning them over a few times so that they brown evenly. Drain on kitchen paper.
To serve: Arrange the langoustines in pyjamas in the centre of the plates and garnish with the fried basil. Serve the mango sauce in a small bowl, on the side.

Home-Made Tagliatelle with Goose Liver

In my opinion, this beats most other pasta dishes. The flavours of the pasta and goose liver meld together extremely well. I like to add some peas, but other green vegetables are equally good in this dish. A crisp salad makes the perfect partner.

SERVES 4

½ onion, finely chopped
2 tbsp olive oil
2 garlic cloves, crushed
½ tsp crushed black peppercorns
50ml/2fl oz/¼ cup white wine vinegar
100ml/3½fl oz/scant ½ cup dry white wine
50ml/2fl oz/¼ cup double (heavy) cream
40g/1½oz goose liver trimmings
450g/1lb tagliatelle (see Ravioli Dough, page 186)
4 x 50g/2oz slices of goose liver
80g/3oz/¾ cup young peas
salt, sea salt and freshly ground black pepper

To make the sauce: Sweat the onion in the olive oil until soft and translucent, then add the garlic and crushed peppercorns and sweat for another minute. Add the vinegar and reduce it completely, then add the white wine and reduce to a syrup. Add the cream and goose liver trimmings, simmer gently for 5 minutes, then pass through a fine sieve and season with salt and pepper.
Cook the tagliatelle in fast-boiling salted water until al dente, then refresh under cold water and drain. Put the tagliatelle in a pan, add the sauce, heat through, and season.
Season the slices of goose liver with sea salt and plenty of black pepper. Heat a non-stick frying pan (skillet) until hot, add the liver, and fry until cooked medium, and browned on both sides. Remove the liver from the pan and season again with freshly ground black pepper.
To serve: Add the peas to the tagliatelle and season. Divide the pasta among 4 bowls and top with the slices of goose liver.

Asparagus and Summer Truffle Salad with Mascarpone

I love the different flavours and contrasting textures of white and green asparagus. In Britain, we traditionally prefer the green spears, and the white variety is not very popular, although it is now readily available. Contrary to what many believe, summer truffles are not the poor cousins of the winter truffle; they are entirely different, with a delicate and gentle flavour that is excellent with vegetables or fish.

SERVES 4

8 white asparagus spears
1 tsp sugar
8 green asparagus spears
4 long chives, blanched
100g/3½oz mature (sharp) Parmesan cheese
4 tsp olive oil
50g/2oz/¼ cup mascarpone cheese
12g/½oz summer truffle, thinly sliced
1 handful of frisée lettuce, yellow leaves only, trimmed, washed and dried
1 handful of wild rocket (arugula) leaves, washed and dried
3 tbsp Lemon Dressing (see page 182)
2½ tbsp Basil Oil (see page 182)
2 tbsp aged, thick balsamic vinegar
salt and freshly ground pepper

Peel the white asparagus very carefully right up to the head. Break off the last 1–2cm/½–¾in of the stalk ends to see whether they are woody. If so, shorten the stalks.
Tie the white asparagus spears into a bundle and boil in salted water with a little added sugar until tender. Refresh in iced water and drain. Peel the green asparagus to about halfway up the stalk. Tie the spears into a bundle and cook in boiling salted water until al dente. Refresh in iced water and drain.
Remove the string from the asparagus. Make 4 bundles of mixed white and green spears, and tie each bundle with a blanched chive. Using a peeler, make 12–14 Parmesan shavings and grate the rest. Heat the olive oil in a wide pan. Add the asparagus bundles and season with salt and pepper and a little of the grated Parmesan. Toss gently in the oil and warm through until tepid.
Put the asparagus bundles on plates. Use 2 teaspoons to shape the mascarpone into small quenelles and place 1 on each plate. Add 3 or 4 summer truffle slices.
Toss the salad leaves (greens) in a little lemon dressing and place beside the asparagus. Top with the Parmesan shavings. Mix the basil oil with the balsamic vinegar and drizzle it over the asparagus.

Duck, Wild Mushroom and Herb Sausages on Lentil Ragoût with Rosemary Mash

Sausages are without doubt an English passion. Over the years at The Savoy, we have played around with these old favourites, and have a hundred and one varieties.

SERVES 4

FOR THE LENTIL RAGOÛT

200g/7oz/scant 1 cup Puy lentils
1 small onion, finely chopped
4 tsp oil
2 garlic cloves, crushed
½ small carrot, finely diced
¼ leek, white part only, washed and finely diced
1 tbsp tomato purée (paste)
50ml/2fl oz/¼ cup sherry vinegar
100ml/3½fl oz/scant ½ cup port
400ml/14fl oz/1¾ cups Chicken Stock (see page 180)

FOR THE SAUSAGES

4 duck thighs, boned and skinned
1 egg white
300ml/10fl oz/1¼ cups double (heavy) cream
2 confit duck legs, skinned, boned and diced (see page 116)
salt and freshly ground pepper

FOR SERVING

2 tbsp oil
50g/2oz/¼ cup unsalted (sweet) butter
100g/3½oz wild mushrooms (chanterelles, girolles, black trumpets, ceps, or a mixture), trimmed, washed and blanched
2 tbsp flat parsley leaves, washed and shredded
350g/12oz Rosemary Mash (see recipe right)

Soak the lentils in cold water for 30 minutes, then rinse, change the water and soak again.

To make the sausages: Mince (grind) the duck thighs through the very fine plate of a mincer (grinder), or whizz to a very fine paste in a food processor, then rub through a drum sieve into a bowl. Stand the bowl on ice and gradually stir in the egg white. Add the cream, a little at a time, then stir in the duck confit. Push the mixture into 8 sausage casings, tie them up, and cook the sausages in simmering water for 15 minutes. Gently remove them and refresh in iced water. When the sausages have cooled, peel off the skins.

To make the lentil ragoût: In a pan, sweat the chopped onion in the oil until soft and translucent, add the garlic and sweat for another minute. Remove 1 tablespoon of the onion and garlic, and reserve. Add the diced carrot and the leek to the rest of the onion mixture, then add the tomato purée (paste) and caramelize for 3–4 minutes, stirring constantly. Drain the lentils and add them to the pan, pour in the vinegar and reduce it completely. Add half the port and the chicken stock, season lightly with salt and pepper, and simmer over very low heat until tender. Take care not to let the lentils dry out; if necessary, add more stock. When the lentils are cooked, adjust the seasoning.

To serve: Fry the sausages in the oil and a little butter until browned all over. Take them out of the pan, add the remaining butter, then the wild mushrooms with the reserved onion and garlic, toss to heat through, season with salt and pepper, and add the shredded parsley. Spoon some lentils on to each plate, top with the sausages, and garnish with the wild mushrooms. Serve with the rosemary mash on the side.

ROSEMARY MASH

MAKES ABOUT 600G/1¼LB

200ml/7fl oz/scant 1 cup olive oil
25g/1oz rosemary
600g/1¼lb potatoes (eg: Maris Piper), peeled and cut into even pieces
6 garlic cloves, peeled
2 tbsp warm milk
50ml/2fl oz/¼ cup double (heavy) cream
salt and freshly ground pepper

Heat the oil and rosemary very gently for about 30 minutes, then strain the oil through a fine sieve.
Cover the potatoes with cold water, add the garlic and salt to taste, and simmer for about 20 minutes until the potatoes are tender. Drain well, return them to the pan, and dry them out over low heat for 5 minutes. Pass the potatoes through a fine sieve or potato ricer, then gradually add the rosemary oil, milk and cream, mixing well. Season with salt and pepper.

Omelette Arnold Bennett

The great writer Arnold Bennett stayed at The Savoy for several months in 1929, researching the backstage workings of the Savoy Hotel Group, on which he based his 1930 novel *Imperial Palace*. This omelette was created for him. He was so delighted that he demanded that chefs made it for him wherever he travelled; it has now become an international favourite. At The Savoy we always make it with the Scottish delicacy finnan haddie, but if this is hard to find, use undyed smoked haddock instead.

MAKES 4 INDIVIDUAL OMELETTES

300g/11oz smoked finnan haddock fillets, skinned
300ml/10fl oz/1¼ cups milk
12 eggs
40g/1½oz/3 tbsp unsalted (sweet) butter
300ml/10fl oz/1¼ cups Béchamel Sauce (see page 183)
5 tbsp Hollandaise Sauce (see page 183)
3 tbsp double (heavy) cream, lightly whipped
1½ tbsp grated Parmesan cheese
salt and freshly ground pepper

Heat the grill (broiler) to high. Poach the finnan haddock in the milk and an equal quantity of water for about 3 minutes. Remove from the pan, drain and flake the fish.
Lightly whisk the eggs, then add half the smoked haddock, and season to taste.
Heat a 20cm/8in omelette pan, add one-quarter of the butter and swirl it around the pan to coat it. Add one-quarter of the egg mixture and cook very quickly, stirring constantly with a fork or spatula until the mixture is lightly set. Slide the omelette out on to a plate.
Quickly mix the Béchamel and Hollandaise sauces together. Add the remaining flaked haddock and carefully fold in the whipped cream. Cover the omelette completely with one-quarter of the sauce. Sprinkle with one-quarter of the Parmesan and glaze under the hot grill until lightly browned. Make 3 more omelettes in the same way and serve immediately.

Linguini with Scallops, Tomatoes and Parsley

I never tire of this very Italian classic pasta dish. The combination of scallops – including the corals or roes – chillies and flat parsley is subtle and quite unusual, and makes a wonderful appetizer or a light main course served with a crisp salad. Good delicatessans sell excellent fresh pasta.

SERVES 4

2 shallots, finely chopped
200 ml/7fl oz/scant 1 cup olive oil
1 garlic clove, finely chopped
½ fresh chilli, de-seeded and chopped
300ml/10fl oz/1¼ cups dry white wine
600g/1¼lb black linguini
2 scallop roes, finely diced
2 plum tomatoes, peeled, de-seeded and diced
a small handful of flat parsley, leaves picked off,
  washed and finely shredded
2 scallops, halved horizontally
salt and freshly ground pepper

Sweat the shallots in 2 tbsp of the olive oil until translucent, then add the garlic and chilli, and sweat for another minute. Add the white wine and reduce by two-thirds.
Cook the linguini in plenty of fast-boiling salted water until *al dente*, then drain and refresh under cold water.
Heat 2 tbsp of the remaining oil in a pan, put in the diced scallop roes, and sweat for 30 seconds. Add the linguini, shallot mixture and tomatoes, and season with salt and pepper. Stir in the shredded parsley and half the remaining olive oil.
Season the halved scallops with salt and pepper. Heat the rest of the olive oil in a non-stick frying pan and quickly sear the scallops for about 15 seconds on each side. Divide the linguini among 4 warmed soup plates, and top with the scallops.

Magically Quick Pizza on Wholemeal (Whole-wheat) Pitta

This snack is quick to make and very versatile. When our children were small, this was always a winner with them and their mother, who loved the fact that it requires so little work. It features on our room service menu and is also popular with our post-theatre customers, who want a quick bite in the Upstairs Restaurant before setting off for home. The sauce base can be made in advance and kept in the refrigerator for 4 or 5 days.

SERVES 4

FOR THE BASE SAUCE

1 onion, chopped
3 tbsp olive oil
2 garlic cloves, crushed
½ tbsp tomato purée (paste)
400g/14oz can chopped tomatoes, drained
100ml/3½fl oz/scant ½ cup Chicken Stock (see page 180)
½ tsp dried oregano
salt and freshly ground pepper

1 mozzarella, preferably buffalo
½ chorizo sausage
1 large tomato
4 wholemeal (whole-wheat) pittas
15g/½oz/½ cup fresh basil leaves

To make the sauce base: Sweat the onions in olive oil until translucent, add the garlic and sweat for another minute, then add the tomato purée (paste), and caramelize for a few minutes. Add the tomatoes, chicken stock and oregano, and simmer until reduced to a paste. Season with salt and pepper. Leave to cool and chill until ready to use.
To make the pizzas: Heat the oven to 200°C/400°F/Gas Mark 6. Slice the mozzarella, chorizo and tomato. Spread a generous amount of sauce base over the pittas and top with the mozzarella, chorizo and sliced tomato. Put the pizzas on a baking tray (cookie sheet) and bake for 15 minutes. A few minutes before the end, divide the basil leaves among the pizzas and bake for another couple of minutes. The heat will bring out the flavour and aroma of the basil.

Smoked Baby Eel Fillets with Beetroot (Beet) and Potato Salad in Horseradish Cream

Baby eels are a great delicacy, but are sadly only appreciated by a select few who understand and love exceptional morsels. The combination of beetroot (beets), potatoes and horseradish in this salad is to die for. If you can't find baby eel fillets, use good quality mature fillets or smoked salmon instead.

SERVES 4

3–4 raw beetroot (beets)
200g/7oz new potatoes
1 tbsp olive oil
1 tsp ground cumin
2 tbsp Mayonnaise (see page 183)
4 tbsp crème fraîche
3 tbsp snipped chives
4 tbsp freshly grated horseradish
4 smoked fillets of baby eel
1 tsp oscietra caviar (optional)
3 tbsp Lemon Dressing (see page 182)
2 tsp Beetroot (Beet) Glaze (see page 138)
salt and freshly ground pepper

First cook the beetroot (beets) and potatoes. Heat the oven to 200°C/400°F/Gas Mark 6. Wrap the beetroot in foil, add a few drops of olive oil, and bake in the oven for 50 minutes or until tender.
Meanwhile, boil the new potatoes in salted water with the cumin until tender. Drain them and peel while still warm, and cut them in half. Take the cooked beetroot out of the foil, peel and cut them into even triangles about the same size as the potatoes. Leave to cool.
To make the potato salad: Mix the potatoes with the mayonnaise and crème fraîche, add the chives, season with salt and pepper, and finally stir in the horseradish.
To serve: Make a mound of potato salad in the middle of each plate. Cut the baby eel fillets into about 20 slices, arrange 5 slices on top of the potato salad on each plate, and top with a little caviar if you like. Toss the beetroot in the lemon dressing and arrange it around the edge. Drizzle with beetroot glaze.

Savoy Fishcakes with Tomato Rösti

Fishcakes seem to be just about everybody's favourite food. Over the last 20 years we have come up with many different recipes and garnishes, but I think we will stick with this excellent version, which makes the perfect light meal. The fishcakes are bound with just a little mayonnaise and breadcrumbs, and are very light and easy to eat. They are so popular with our customers that we feature them on both the supper and lunch menus.

SERVES 4

100g/3½oz salmon fillet, skinned and pin bones removed
100g/3½oz whiting fillet, skinned and pin bones removed
100g/3½oz cod fillet, skinned and pin bones removed
25g/1oz gherkins, chopped
25g/1oz/⅓ cup finely chopped spring onion (scallion)
½ fresh chilli, de-seeded and finely chopped
3 tbsp Mayonnaise (see page 183)
1 tsp chopped fresh root ginger
80g/3oz/1½ cups fresh white breadcrumbs
salt and freshly ground pepper

FOR THE TOMATO RÖSTI

400g/14oz Maris Piper potatoes, unpeeled
3 vine tomatoes
2 tbsp oil

FOR THE GARNISH

1 handful each of rocket (arugula) and frisée lettuce
2 tbsp Lemon Dressing (see page 182)
4 dried tomato rings
200ml/7fl oz/scant 1 cup White Wine Sauce (see page 184)
½ tsp wholegrain mustard
1 tsp shredded flat parsley

To make the fishcakes: Prepare a steamer, put all the fish in the top, and steam for about 3 minutes. Cover with cling film (plastic wrap) and cool quickly.

Flake the fish and mix with the gherkins, spring onion (scallion), chilli, mayonnaise, ginger and one-third of the breadcrumbs. Season with salt and pepper. Put the remaining breadcrumbs in a dish, then put in the fish mixture and shape it with a palette knife (metal spatula) into 4 cylindrical shapes, about 4cm/1½in high and 6cm/2½ in wide (about 100g/3½oz each). Make sure they are well coated with breadcrumbs. Chill the fishcakes for 30 minutes to firm them up.

To make the tomato rösti: Wash the potatoes well and steam for about 15 minutes until half-cooked, then peel, cool and grate them. Season with salt and pepper, and mix well.

Slice the tomatoes. Grease four 10 cm/4 in rösti tins (pans) with a film of oil and divide the end pieces of the tomatoes among them. Alternatively, place four 10 cm/4 in pastry (cookie) cutters in a large lightly oiled frying pan (skillet). Fill with the grated potatoes and fry over high heat until crispy, then turn the rösti and fry on the other side.

To cook the fishcakes: Heat the oven to 220°C/425°F/Gas Mark 7. Heat a little oil in a non-stick frying pan, and fry the fishcakes until golden brown on both sides. Transfer the pan to the oven for about 6 minutes, until the fishcakes are heated through.

To serve: Arrange a ring of sliced vine tomatoes on each plate, top with the rösti, and put the fishcakes on top. Toss the rocket (arugula) in the lemon dressing, place it on top of the fishcakes, and arrange the dried tomato slices on top.

Heat the white wine sauce, add the mustard and shredded parsley, and pour the sauce around the fishcakes.

Savoy Burgers with Fried Eggs and Tomato Relish

A universally popular supper dish. Serve with fried eggs or without.

SERVES 4

FOR THE BURGERS

100g/3½oz/scant ½ cup finely chopped onions
4 tbsp olive oil
4 garlic cloves, crushed
2 bread rolls, cut into thin slices and soaked in milk
400g/14oz rump (round) of beef, all fat removed, cubed
200g/7oz shoulder of pork, cubed
7 organic eggs
salt and freshly ground pepper

FOR THE DEEP-FRIED ONION RINGS

80g/3oz/⅔ cup plain (all-purpose) flour
3 tbsp paprika
1 onion, cut into 3mm/⅛in rings
100ml/3½fl oz/scant ½ cup milk
oil, for deep-frying

FOR THE TOMATO RELISH

1 red onion, finely chopped
½ fresh chilli, de-seeded and finely diced
3 tomatoes, peeled, de-seeded and diced
3 tbsp flat parsley leaves, washed and shredded
pinch of ground cumin
1 tsp white wine vinegar

To make the burgers: Sweat the onions in the olive oil until soft, add the garlic and sweat for another minute. Transfer to a large bowl and leave to cool. Squeeze out the milk from the bread rolls. Mince (grind) the beef and pork, and mix all the meat with the cooked onion mixture and the bread. Add 3 eggs and work them in until well mixed, and season with salt and pepper. Shape into 4 burgers and place them in the refrigerator to firm up.
To make the fried onion rings: Mix the flour and paprika. Dip the onion rings in the milk, then turn them in the flour mixture to coat them all over, and shake off the excess flour. Heat the oil to 160°C/320°F and deep-fry the onion rings until golden brown.
To make the tomato relish: Mix all the ingredients.
To serve: Grill (broil) or fry the burgers until done to your liking. Fry the remaining 4 eggs in the remaining olive oil, put them on top of the burgers, and serve with the onion rings and tomato relish.

Vegetable Risotto with Rocket (Arugula) and Parmesan Shavings

The addition of rocket (arugula) on the risotto gives a contrasting crunchiness, while the lemon dressing adds a touch of acidity which I think works very well.

SERVES 4

600ml/1 pint/2½ cups Vegetable Stock (see page 182),
  or Chicken Stock (see page 180)
1 onion, finely chopped
50ml/2fl oz/¼ cup olive oil
100g/3½oz carrots, peeled and finely diced
100g/3½oz fennel, peeled and finely diced
100g/3½oz courgettes (zucchini), finely diced (use only the green skin side, not the soft white inside)
120g/4oz/1 cup risotto rice
100ml/3½fl oz/scant ½ cup dry white wine
12 cherry tomatoes
15g/½oz/½ cup basil leaves
40g/1½ oz/½ cup freshly grated Parmesan cheese
50g/2oz/¼ cup unsalted (sweet) butter
salt and freshly ground pepper

FOR THE GARNISH

2 handfuls of rocket (arugula), optional
2 tbsp Lemon Dressing (see page 182), optional
Parmesan cheese shavings

Heat the vegetable or chicken stock almost to boiling point.
In a pan, sweat the onion in the olive oil until soft and translucent. Add the diced vegetables and sweat for 1 minute.
Add the rice and stir until all the grains are coated in the oil, then add half the wine and cook until it has almost evaporated.
Add enough hot stock to cover the rice, and simmer over very low heat. As the rice absorbs the stock, add a little more, keeping the rice just covered with the stock. Continue cooking in this way for 15–20 minutes, adding the stock little by little, and stirring frequently.
Meanwhile, heat the grill (broiler). Cut the cherry tomatoes in half and shred the basil leaves. Sprinkle the basil over the tomatoes and sprinkle on a little grated Parmesan. Cook under the hot grill (broiler) until the tomatoes are soft.
When the rice is nearly done, add the remaining Parmesan and the remaining wine, and season with salt and pepper. Beat in the butter. Serve the risotto in soup plates and arrange the cherry tomatoes on top. Toss the rocket (arugula) in the lemon dressing and place a little on top of the risotto. Top with the Parmesan shavings.

Vegetarian Club Sandwiches

Vegetarians are on the increase and even non-vegetarians like myself try to fit in meat-free days. I always feel better for this, and I am sure Savoy customers do too. This vegetarian club sandwich is certainly always a winner.

SERVES 4

8 garlic cloves
100ml/3½fl oz/scant ½ cup olive oil
1 courgette (zucchini), cut into paper-thin slices
1 aubergine (eggplant), cut into paper-thin slices
½ red (bell) pepper, de-seeded and cut into 1cm/½in wide strips
1 fennel bulb, cut into paper-thin slices
2 Little Gem (Bibb) lettuces
3 tbsp Mayonnaise (see page 183)
4 x 5mm/¼in thick slices of sourdough bread
2 hard-boiled (hard-cooked) eggs, peeled and thinly sliced
2 vine tomatoes, thinly sliced
8 basil leaves, washed and shredded
½ red onion, thinly sliced
100g/3½oz hummus
40g/1½oz/⅓ cup mixed olives, to garnish

First roast the garlic: Heat the oven to 200°C/400°F/Gas Mark 6. Separate the garlic cloves and put them on a piece of foil. Add a drizzle of olive oil, wrap the garlic in the foil, and bake in the oven for about 45 minutes until soft. Squeeze out the flesh from 4 of the cloves and mash them. Reserve the other 4 garlic cloves. Heat a griddle pan or the grill (broiler) until very hot. Turn the sliced courgette (zucchini), aubergine (eggplant), (bell) pepper and fennel in a little oil and griddle or grill (broil) to mark them on both sides. Put the remaining oil in a pan and simmer the vegetables until tender, then take them out of the oil and drain well.
Cut the lettuces in half, then into thin slices. Wash and dry them, and mix with the mayonnaise and crushed roasted garlic.
Lightly toast the bread. Put a spoonful of the lettuce mixture on one slice, then a layer of egg, some tomato and basil and a little red onion. Top with another slice of toasted bread and spread on some hummus. Make a layer of grilled vegetables and finally top with the remaining slice of toast. Repeat to make 3 more club sandwiches. Cut each one into triangles and garnish with the reserved garlic and the olives.

The American Bar

The legendary American Bar at The Savoy has the elegant feel of the saloon of a 1930s ocean liner in its heyday. Mirrored walls, rounded columns and porthole-like lights lead you towards the prow, where the "captain" (barman) shakes and stirs the cocktails for which the bar is famous.

Tucked away behind a pillar is the "Royal Box", a cosy area reserved for parties. Here the view of the river with boats passing by reinforces the impression of being at sea.

The Savoy American Bar was not the first of its kind to open in London, but it is probably the oldest still in existence. Its name does not relate to its popularity as a watering hole for transatlantic visitors. "American" is the generic term for a bar specializing in mixed drinks; these were the first bars to serve cocktails chilled or "on the rocks" – a concept unheard of in Europe, but de rigueur in America.

Until the original American Bar opened in 1898, The Savoy had no area where men and women could enjoy a drink together – it was not socially acceptable for "nice" women to drink in public. Despite this, the first of the hotel's long line of famous bartenders was a barmaid, Ada Coleman (affectionately known as "Coley"), whose twenty-one year tenure in the American Bar lasted from 1903 until 1924. Her best-known creation was the Hanky Panky, which she invented for Sir Charles Hawtrey, but she was also noted for her lethal-sounding Midnight Cocktail, which contained a good dash of absinthe. This was highly popular with guests who came to dance at The Savoy, but how they could stand up afterwards, let alone dance, remains a mystery.

By 1920, the American Bar had moved to its present location behind the lobby, and its most famous barman, Harry Craddock (in picture opposite), was hired from New York. He was followed by a flock of thirsty Americans who eagerly migrated to London to escape Prohibition. A teetotaller himself, Craddock always tasted the cocktails he created, but he never swallowed them. He could (and did) devise a cocktail to mark any and every occasion, from the end of the General Strike to the Earthquake Cocktail ("so-called because if there should happen to be an earthquake while you are drinking it, it won't matter"). In 1930, his definitive *Savoy Cocktail Book* was published, containing descriptions of every conceivable cocktail of the time, including his own most famous invention, the White Lady.

Small wonder that his successor Eddie Clark, promoted the definitive cure for over-indulgence. His boast was that one of his Prairie Oysters would chase away most hangovers, while two would assure you that the pink elephant that had been following you around all day belonged to the fellow sitting on the next bar stool!

The present head barman, Peter Dorelli, continues the custom of concocting cocktails for special occasions, from the Moonwalk to the 1889'er, which he created for the Savoy's Centenary in 1989 – a fitting tribute to the best American Bar of them all.

Malibu Froth With Exotic Fruits

This dessert may be modest, but it has plenty of "oomph" and wit.
It is often often served at The Savoy as a pre-dessert or at
functions, as the combination of blackcurrant and passion fruit is
great for clearing the palate, and the hint of Malibu gets you in the
mood for more.

100ml/3½fl oz/scant ½ cup blackcurrant purée
1 gelatine leaf
1 tbsp each of: mango, peeled, stoned (pitted) and diced; kiwi fruit,
   peeled and diced; papaya) peeled , de-seeded and diced; dragon
   fruit, peeled and diced

FOR THE PASSION FRUIT SORBET (SHERBET)

150ml/5fl oz/⅔ cup passion fruit purée
15g/½oz/1 tbsp sugar
150ml/5fl oz/⅔ cup water
1 tbsp liquid glucose
zest of ½ lime

FOR THE MALIBU FROTH

150ml/5fl oz/⅔ cup milk
25g/1oz/2 tbsp sugar
4 tsp Malibu liqueur

To make the passion fruit sorbet (sherbet): Combine the passion
fruit purée with the sugar, water, liquid glucose and lime zest, and
churn in an ice cream maker until set.
Heat the blackcurrant purée. Soak the gelatine leaf, squeeze out
the water, and stir into the hot blackcurrant purée. Divide the purée
between 4 small espresso cups, and chill for 1 hour until set.
To serve: Divide the exotic fruit mixture between the cups. Make the
Malibu froth by heating the milk, sugar and Malibu to 70°C/158°F.
Put a spoonful of passion fruit sorbet on top of the fruit, then whizz
up the milk with a hand-held blender and spoon this froth all over
the sorbet to cover it completely.

Petits Parfaits Glacés Paquita

This is my revamped version of a very old Savoy classic. I am delighted with the result, as I think it fits in very nicely with the Art Deco style of The Savoy

SERVES 4

3 egg yolks
3 tbsp anisette liqueur
250g/9oz/1¼ cups caster (superfine) sugar
200ml/7fl oz/scant 1 cup double (heavy) cream
25g/1oz/¼ cup hazelnuts, roasted, skinned and finely chopped
20g/¾oz Sponge Cake (see recipe right)
1½ tbsp kirsch
4 egg whites
50g/2oz orange segments
50g/2oz papaya) cut into lozenges
50g/2oz kiwi fruit, cut into lozenges

FOR THE RASPBERRY SAUCE

300g/11oz/scant 2 cups raspberries
2 tsp lemon juice
40g/1½ oz/⅓ cup icing (confectioners') sugar

To make the raspberry sauce: Whizz the raspberries in a blender, then add the lemon juice and icing (confectioners') sugar. Pass through a fine sieve or muslin (cheesecloth).
For the parfaits: Put the egg yolks, anisette and 40g/1½oz/¼ cup of the caster (superfine) sugar in a heatproof bowl, and whisk over boiling water to form a light, fluffy sabayon. Remove from heat and whisk until cool.
Lightly whip the cream, and fold in the hazelnuts and sabayon. Spoon this mixture into 4 dariole moulds (about 5cm/2in diameter and 7.5cm/3in high). Cover with cling film (plastic wrap) and freeze until firm.
Cut the sponge cake into four 5cm/2in rounds and moisten with the kirsch. Dip the dariole moulds into hot water and unmould the parfaits on to the sponge rounds. Place on chilled freezerproof and heatproof plates and put them in the freezer. Heat the grill (broiler) to high.
To make the meringue: Whisk the egg whites until stiff, then whisk in the remaining caster sugar, a spoonful at a time until the mixture is thick and glossy. Put the meringue in a piping (pastry) bag fitted with a small star nozzle (tip), and pipe the meringue up the sides of each parfait to cover it completely. Glaze evenly under the hot grill until light golden brown.

To serve: arrange the fruit on the plates and serve the raspberry sauce separately.

SPONGE CAKE

MAKES ABOUT 700G/1½LB

butter, for greasing
10 large (extra large) eggs, beaten
2 large (extra large) egg yolks
400g/14oz/2 cups caster (superfine) sugar
250g/9oz/2¼ cups plain (all-purpose) flour, sifted

Heat the oven to 230°C/450°F/Gas Mark 8. Butter 2 large baking trays (cookie sheets) and line with greaseproof (waxed) paper. Put the beaten eggs and yolks with the sugar in an electric mixer and whisk at high speed for 7 minutes, then at slow speed for 3 minutes. Fold in the flour. Spread a thin layer of the mixture on to the prepared trays and bake immediately in the hot oven for about 5 minutes. Leave the sponges to cool on the trays, then gently peel off the lining paper.

Pêches Nellie Melba

Escoffier created this dish for the great Australian opera singer Dame Nellie Melba in the late nineteenth century. Inspired by her performance in the opera *Lohengrin*, Escoffier served the dessert set into a swan carved out of ice. We prepared it in its original form for the late Queen Mother when she lunched in The Savoy Restaurant to celebrate The Savoy's centenary in 1989. After that lunch, she opened the newly refurbished kitchen, which inspired me to recreate Escoffier's Peach Melba; this is my somewhat less flamboyant (but no less delectable) version of his classic dish.

SERVES 4

2 large peaches
300ml/10fl oz/1¼ cups Raspberry Sauce (see page 185)
4 tuile baskets (see recipe right)
400ml/14fl oz/1½ cups Vanilla Ice Cream (see page 188)

FOR THE SUGAR SYRUP

500g/1lb 2oz/2½ cups caster (superfine) sugar
1 litre/1¾ pints/4 cups water
50ml/2fl oz/¼ cup lemon juice

FOR THE SPUN SUGAR CAGES

250g/9oz/1¼ cups caster (superfine) sugar
100ml/3½fl oz/scant ½ cup water
10g/¼oz liquid glucose

First make the sugar syrup: Dissolve the sugar in the water over a medium heat. Add the lemon juice and bring to the boil. Leave to cool and strain before using.
To prepare the peaches: Poach them in the sugar syrup for 1 minute until you can peel off the skin easily. Peel, leave to cool, then cut in half and remove the stones (pits).
To make the spun sugar cages: Mix the sugar, water and glucose together in a small pan and set over a high heat. Brush the sides of the pan quite frequently with a little water to prevent crystallization. Cook the sugar to the hard crack stage (168°C/336°F on a sugar thermometer), then turn off the heat and leave until the syrup becomes thick. Oil the outside of a 10cm/4in diameter ladle. Dip 2 dessert forks in the sugar syrup and flick very fine threads over the upturned ladle, changing the direction of the threads to form a lattice effect. Turn the ladle on its side and finish with a thin line of sugar syrup around the edge of the ladle to form the base of the cage. As soon as it is cool, carefully remove the cage from the ladle and keep in a cool, dry place. Make 3 more cages in the same way.
To serve: Pour a little of the raspberry sauce on to 4 plates. Place a tuile basket in the middle of each plate. Scoop one-quarter of the vanilla ice cream into the centre, set a peach half on top, and spoon over a little raspberry sauce. Carefully arrange a sugar cage on top of each tuile basket.

TUILE BASKETS

100g/3½oz/scant 1 cup plain flour
100g/3½oz/scant 1 cup icing (confectioners') sugar
100g/3½oz/scant ½ cup unsalted (sweet) butter, melted
2 egg whites
flaked (sliced) almonds, to decorate

Sift the flour and icing (confectioners') sugar into a mixing bowl. Quickly stir in the melted butter and egg whites to make a smooth paste. Chill for 30 minutes.
Heat the oven to 190°C/375°F/Gas Mark 5. Place an eight-pointed 12.5cm/5in diameter star-shaped plastic stencil on a buttered and floured baking tray (cookie sheet). Spread a little tuile mixture in the centre and draw a palette knife (metal spatula) evenly over the surface. Remove the stencil and make 3 more stars in the same way. Sprinkle a few flaked almonds in the centre of each star. Bake in the oven for 4–5 minutes until light brown.
While the tuiles are still hot, place each in a small glass bowl to form a basket. Leave in the bowls until cold and crisp.

Pannacotta with Lavender and Rhubarb Compote

Every chef seems to feature a pannacotta in some guise or other. This is my version, which has an unexpected twist. It's extremely light and has to be made at least 12 hours in advance. You need a very delicate touch when you turn it out of the mould, but the delicate flavour makes the effort worthwhile.

SERVES 4

3 gelatine leaves
300ml/10fl oz/1¼ cups double (heavy) cream
2 tbsp dried lavender flowers, chopped
2 vanilla pods (beans), split lengthways, and scraped
100ml/3½fl oz/scant ½ cup condensed milk
350ml/12fl oz/1½ cups buttermilk, at room temperature
100g/3½ oz/½ cup caster (superfine) sugar
4 Tuiles (see page 67). to decorate

FOR THE RHUBARB COMPOTE

400g/14oz rhubarb, peeled and cut into 2cm/1in sticks
juice of ½ lemon
1 cinnamon stick
1 clove
50ml/2fl oz/¼ cup Stock Syrup (see page 185)

To make the pannacotta: Soak the gelatine leaves in a little cold water for about 4 minutes, then squeeze out the water. Heat the cream with the lavender and vanilla pods (beans). When it comes to the boil, take off the heat and stir in the condensed milk and gelatine. Cool to blood temperature, then stir in the buttermilk, strain through a fine sieve and pour into four 8cm/3¼in ramekins. Reserve the vanilla pods for the rhubarb compote. Chill the pannacotta for at least 6 hours, or better still overnight (it will be very delicate).

To make the rhubarb compote: Put the rhubarb, lemon juice, cinnamon stick, clove and stock syrup in a pan, scrape in the seeds from the reserved vanilla pods, and simmer till the rhubarb is very soft. Cool, remove the cinnamon,vanilla pod and clove and cut it into long, thin slivers.

To serve: Quickly dip the ramekins in hot water and unmould the pannacotta on to serving plates. Arrange the rhubarb compote around and decorate with tuiles.

Gooseberry Crumbles with
Chocolate Orange Ripple

Gooseberries tend to be sadly ignored nowadays, which I think is a great shame. When picked at the right time, they are full of flavour and character and have their own very distinctive taste. In a bad British summer, however, they will never develop any sweetness, which is when this crumble comes in useful. The chocolate orange ripple is not essential, but adds an extra special something.

SERVES 4

200g/7oz gooseberries
100ml/3½fl oz/scant ½ cup Stock Syrup (see page 185)
1 vanilla pod (bean), split lengthways
¼ fresh green chilli
¼ tsp five-spice powder
4 x 10cm/4in baked tartlet cases (shells) in their moulds
 (see Passion Fruit Tart, page 66)
4 orange segments, all pith removed

FOR THE CRUMBLE

170g/6oz/1½ cups plain (all-purpose) flour
50g/2oz/¼ cup soft dark brown sugar
50g/2oz/⅓ cup caster (superfine) sugar
80g/3oz/6 tbsp unsalted (sweet) butter
20g/1½oz/⅓ cup ground almonds

FOR THE CHOCOLATE ORANGE RIPPLE
200ml/7fl oz/scant 1 cup orange juice
40g/1½oz/scant ¼ cup soft dark brown sugar
1 tbsp honey
½ vanilla pod (bean), split lengthways
200g/7oz/scant 1 cup Vanilla Ice Cream (see page 188)
150g/5oz plain (semisweet) cooking chocolate or couverture, melted

Start by making the chocolate orange ripple: Reduce the orange juice with the brown sugar, honey and vanilla pod (bean) by at least one-third, until slightly thickened. Leave to cool.
Divide the ice cream between 2 bowls. Mix the melted chocolate into half the vanilla ice cream, and the orange reduction with the other half. Roughly ripple the two mixtures in a bowl, place in a 6cm/2¼in triangular mould, and freeze for 2 hours until hardened.
To make the gooseberry crumbles: Heat the oven to 200°C/400°F/Gas Mark 6.
Simmer the gooseberries in the stock syrup with the vanilla pod, chilli and five-spice powder until tender (about 5 minutes), and leave to cool in the syrup. Strain the gooseberries, drain them on kitchen paper (paper towels), and divide them among the pastry cases (shells).
To make the crumble: Mix the flour, brown and caster (superfine) sugars, butter and ground almonds until the mixture resembles fine breadcrumbs, and spread the crumble over the gooseberries. Bake in the oven for about 20 minutes, until the crumble is browned.
To serve: Turn the tartlets out of the moulds and place on warm plates. Unmould the chocolate orange ripple, cut it into four 1.5cm/½in slices or crescents. Place the crescents on top and then an orange segment.

Pineapple Pot-Pourri

Although they were once an exotic luxury, nowadays pineapples are very cheap and readily available, yet we rarely see them used in a pudding. I consider this a sad oversight, since a really ripe pineapple has a flavour second to none. This recipe was created for the "Other Club", the famous dining club started by Winston Churchill during the war. Its members are ex-Prime Ministers and senior politicians, who invite the opinion-formers of the nation to a dinner once a month.

SERVES 4

1 ripe pineapple, peeled
2 tbsp Spicy Stock Syrup (see recipe right)

FOR THE PARFAITS

8 egg yolks
250g/9oz/generous 1 cup sugar
300ml/10fl oz/1¼ cups double (heavy) cream,
   whipped to soft peaks
4 tiny mint sprigs, to garnish

For the pineapple rings: Heat the oven to 190°C/375°F/Gas Mark 5. Cut four 1cm/½in thick slices from the pineapple and remove the woody core with a corer or pastry (cookie) cutter. Using a 9cm/3½in cutter, cut each slice into a ring. Place in a shallow ovenproof dish, pour over half the spicy syrup, and bake in the oven for 20 minutes.
To make the pineapple wafers: Reduce the oven temperature to 100°C/212°F or the lowest gas setting. Cut 4 paper-thin slices from the remaining pineapple, core them and cut into 9 cm/3½in rings as before. Dip these into the remaining syrup and place them on a sheet of baking parchment or greaseproof (waxed) paper. Place in the oven, leaving the door open, and leave until dry and golden (about 2 hours).
Cool until brittle.

To make the pineapple purée: Cut 50g/2oz of the remaining pineapple into small dice and purée the rest in a blender. Whisk the eggs yolks in an electric mixer until doubled in volume. Meanwhile, boil the sugar with a little water until it has dissolved completely and is syrupy. With the motor of the food processor still running, add the syrup to the eggs, and whisk until cool. Transfer to a bowl, and fold in the cream and pineapple purée. Pipe the mixture into ramekins or moulds, 8cm/3¼ in wide and 4cm/1½in deep, and freeze.
To serve: Place a pineapple ring on each plate. Turn out the frozen parfaits and set them on top. Arrange a dried pineapple wafer on top of the parfait and decorate with mint sprigs.

SPICY STOCK SYRUP

MAKES 500ML/GENEROUS 2 CUPS

2 vanilla pods (beans)
300g/11oz/1½ cups caster (superfine) sugar
2 bananas, puréed
1 fresh chilli, de-seeded and chopped
20g/¾oz fresh root ginger, peeled and chopped
50ml/2fl oz/¼ cup dark rum
250ml/9fl oz/generous 1 cup water

Split the vanilla pods (beans) lengthways and scrape out the seeds. Combine them with all the other ingredients in a pan.
Bring to the boil and reduce by half. Leave to cool before using.

Welsh Rarebit with Field Mushrooms

I was surprised to discover that the original Welsh rarebit doesn't contain any Welsh cheese at all, so I have rectified this and added one. It changes the flavour of this classic savoury and makes it a little sharper, which I think is an improvement. I added the mushrooms to give a more interesting texture.

SERVES 4

20g/¾oz/1½ tbsp butter
50g/2oz/½ cup plain (all-purpose) flour
150ml/5fl oz/⅔ cup milk
150g/6oz/1½ cups grated Cheddar cheese
150g/6oz/1½ cups grated Emmenthal cheese
150g/6oz/1½ cups grated Pencarreg blue
 or similar Welsh blue cheese
1 free-range (farm fresh) egg
2 free-range (farm fresh) egg yolks
1½ tbsp English (hot) mustard
½ tsp Worcestershire sauce
8 large field (portabello) mushrooms
4 slices of sourdough bread
salt and cayenne pepper

First make a roux: Melt the butter in a pan, add the flour, and cook over a medium heat without colouring for 3–4 minutes. Add a little of the milk and stir to make a thick smooth paste. Continue adding a little more milk until it has all been absorbed and the roux is very smooth; if it is at all lumpy, pass it through a fine sieve and return it to the pan. Simmer for 5 minutes, stirring frequently, then add the grated cheeses, and stir until they have melted. Take the pan off the heat.
Whisk the egg and egg yolks and stir into the cheese mixture. Add the mustard, Worcestershire sauce and salt and cayenne to taste.
To prepare the mushrooms: Heat the grill (broiler) to very hot. Bring a pan of salted water to the boil. Peel the mushrooms and trim the stalks. Boil them for 30 seconds, drain, refresh in cold water, and season with salt and pepper. Grill (broil) the mushrooms for 5 minutes.
Toast the bread, top with the mushrooms, and spoon on enough cheese mixture to cover the toast completely. Grill (broil) until lightly browned.

Devilled Kidneys on Toast

This rather old-fashioned and very masculine dish may not appeal to everyone, but personally, I would like to eat it more often. Although it is traditionally served as a savoury after a meal, it also makes an excellent snack. It is equally good made with calves' liver or kidneys.

SERVES 8

8 cherry tomatoes on the vine, halved
1 tbsp flat parsley leaves, shredded
50g/2oz/⅓ cup freshly grated Parmesan cheese
2 shallots, finely chopped
4 tbsp olive oil
1 garlic clove, crushed
6 tbsp fresh white breadcrumbs
8 lamb's kidneys, halved and fat removed
6 slices of olive bread
1 tbsp English (hot) mustard
4 tsp crème fraîche (optional)
salt and freshly ground pepper

Heat the grill (broiler). Put the cherry tomatoes on a heatproof plate, grind on some pepper, and sprinkle with one-third of the shredded parsley and grated Parmesan. Grill (broil) until lightly browned. Leave the grill switched on for the kidneys.
Sweat the shallots in half the oil until translucent, add the garlic and sweat for another minute. Add the breadcrumbs and one-third of the parsley, and season with salt and pepper. Season the kidneys and grill them until cooked to your liking.
Toast the bread and, while it is toasting, remove the kidneys from the grill, brush them with the mustard, and sprinkle the breadcrumb mixture on top.
To serve: Place 2 kidney halves and 2 cherry tomato halves on each slice of toast, top with a teaspoon of crème fraîche if you wish, and sprinkle with the remaining parsley.

Basic Recipes and Side Dishes

Stocks

CHICKEN STOCK

MAKES ABOUT 2.5 LITRES/4½ PINTS/11¼ CUPS

2 x 1.2kg/2½lb chickens
2 onions, coarsely chopped
2 carrots, coarsely chopped
2 celery sticks, coarsely chopped
1 bay leaf
2 thyme sprigs
a few parsley stalks
1 tsp black peppercorns, coarsely crushed
salt

Cut off the chicken breasts and reserve them for another dish. Pull off as much of the skin from the chicken as possible and discard it. Chop the chicken carcasses, wings and leg portions into pieces and put them into a stockpot or large pan. Cover with 3.75 litres/ 6½ pints/16¼ cups cold water and bring slowly to simmering point, skimming often to remove all the froth from the surface. Simmer for 10 minutes, then add the vegetables, herbs, peppercorns and a little salt, and continue to simmer very gently for 1 hour.
Turn up the heat a little so the liquid is simmering a little more quickly, but not boiling. Simmer for a further hour. Strain the stock and leave to cool completely. Remove any fat from the surface before using.

FISH STOCK

MAKES ABOUT 2 LITRES/3½ PINTS/8¾ CUPS

1kg/2¼ sole or turbot bones
40g/1½oz/3 tbsp chopped shallot
20g/¾oz/1½ tbsp unsalted (sweet) butter
200ml/7fl oz/scant 1 cup dry white wine
1 litre/1¾ pints/4 cups water
50g/2oz leeks, sliced
50g/2oz celery, sliced
12 white peppercorns

1 bay leaf
10g/¼oz/¼ cup parsley stalks
20g/¾oz/⅓ cup mushroom trimmings
salt and pepper

Chop the fish bones and wash well in cold water. Sweat the shallots in the butter, add the fish bones, cover and cook for about 3 minutes. Add the white wine, water and the remaining ingredients. Bring to the boil and simmer for about 15 minutes, skimming frequently. Pass through fine muslin (cheesecloth) and skim off any remaining fat.

BEEF STOCK

MAKES ABOUT 2 LITRES/3½ PINTS/8¾ CUPS

1.4kg/3lb beef bones, chopped
675g/1½lb onions, chopped
400g/14oz carrots, chopped
½ garlic bulb, chopped
80g/3oz mixed sage and thyme sprigs
3 bay leaves
10 peppercorns, crushed
40g/1½oz/2½ tbsp tomato purée (paste)
1.5 litres/2½ pints/6¼ cups red wine

Heat the oven to 200°C/400°F/Gas Mark 6. Put the bones in a roasting tin (pan) and roast until dark golden brown. Take care not to burn the bones, or the stock will become bitter. Transfer the bones to a stock pot and discard all the fat.
Add the chopped onions, carrots, garlic, herbs and peppercorns to the roasting pan and fry until golden brown.
Add the tomato purée (paste) and cook for 2–3 minutes.
Add half the wine and reduce it to a glaze. Add the rest and reduce again to a glaze.
Tip the contents of the roasting tin into the stock pot with the bones, cover with cold water and bring to the boil. Simmer for 2 hours, skimming frequently. Pass the stock through a conical sieve into a pan and reduce by one-third.

VEAL JUS

MAKES ABOUT 2 LITRES/3½ PINTS/8¾ CUPS

5 pieces of veal bone
200g/7oz carrots, coarsely chopped
200g/7oz onions, coarsely chopped
200g/7oz leeks, coarsely chopped
200g/7oz celery, coarsely chopped
1 calf's foot
1 garlic clove, chopped
100g/3½oz/scant 6 tbsp tomato purée (paste)
300ml/10fl oz/1¼ cups white wine
2 tsp peppercorns, crushed
a few thyme sprigs
2 bay leaves
100g/3½oz tomato trimmings
salt and freshly ground pepper

Place the veal bones in a large pan of cold water and bring to the boil. Drain and wash well under cold running water. Return the bones to the pan, add half the vegetables and cover with cold water. Simmer for about 4 hours, then strain. Discard the bones. Heat the oven to 220°C/425°F/Gas Mark 7. Chop the calf's foot, place in a roasting tin (pan) and roast in the oven until lightly browned. Add the remaining vegetables, garlic and tomato purée (paste). Roast for 15–20 minutes, stirring occasionally. Add the white wine, prepared stock, peppercorns, herbs and tomato trimmings. Simmer gently, skimming frequently. Reduce by half and pass through a fine sieve or muslin (cheesecloth). Season to taste with salt and pepper.

To make a meat glaze: Reduce the veal jus by boiling it to a very thick, dark syrupy glaze.

SEAFOOD BROTH

MAKES ABOUT 2 LITRES/3½ PINTS/8¾ CUPS

2 tsp saffron threads
200ml/7fl oz/scant 1 cup Chicken Stock (see page 180) or water
8 garlic cloves, unpeeled
100ml/3½fl oz/scant ½ cup olive oil
½ red chilli, de-seeded and very finely diced
2 egg yolks
675g/1½lb fresh mussels
400g/14oz leeks, washed, outside leaves removed, cut into squares
100g/3½oz/scant ½ cup chopped onions
200ml/7fl oz/scant 1 cup dry white wine
200ml/7fl oz/scant 1 cup double (heavy) cream
50g/2oz salmon fillet
2 scallops, halved
50g/2oz halibut
4 tiger prawns (jumbo shrimp), shelled and cut into 5mm/¼in cubes
cayenne pepper
salt and freshly ground pepper

Heat the oven to 200°C/400°F/Gas Mark 6. Put half the saffron with 50ml/2fl oz/¼ cup chicken stock or water in a small pan, and simmer for 2 minutes until reduced by half. Pass through a fine sieve and leave to cool.

Rub 4 garlic cloves with a little olive oil, wrap in foil and roast in the hot oven for about 45 minutes until soft. Remove from the foil and squeeze the garlic out of its skin. Add the garlic, chilli and saffron to the egg yolks and stir in the remaining olive oil. Season.

Thoroughly wash and scrub the mussels under cold running water. Make sure that they are all firmly closed; discard any that are not. Put the mussels, the remaining garlic cloves, 100g/3½oz of the leeks, the onions, white wine and remaining chicken stock or water in a large pan, cover tightly with a lid, and heat very quickly for 2–3 minutes, stirring now and again, until all the mussels are open. Discard any that remain shut.

Strain the cooking liquid through a colander into a tall container. Cover the mussels with a cloth to keep them from drying out.

Slightly tilt the container of mussel stock and let any sand and grit settle on the base. Carefully ladle off the stock from the top into a pan. Remove the mussels from their shells and discard the beards and shells. Add the remaining saffron to the stock, then add the cream and bring to a simmer. Season the fish and shellfish, put them in the stock and simmer for 2 minutes. Season to taste with cayenne pepper.

The garlic, chilli, saffron and egg mixture is served on top of the broth.

Dressings and Chutneys

VEGETABLE STOCK

MAKES ABOUT 1 LITRE/1¾ PINTS/4 CUPS

2 onions, finely chopped
2 tbsp oil
1 small fennel bulb, finely chopped
2 celery sticks, finely chopped
200g/7oz carrots, finely chopped
225g/8oz celeriac (celery root), finely chopped
2 leeks, white and pale green parts only, thinly sliced
1 large garlic clove, sliced
2 star anise
¼ tsp black peppercorns
½ tsp coriander seeds
1 small bay leaf
juice of ½ lime
200ml/7fl oz/scant cup dry white wine
salt

In a large pan, gently sweat the onions with the oil until soft and translucent, stirring frequently. Add the remaining vegetables and 150ml/5fl oz/⅔ cup water. Mix well, then cover and cook gently for about 30 minutes, stirring occasionally. If necessary, add a little more water to prevent the vegetables from sticking to the pan. Meanwhile, coarsely crush the star anise, peppercorns and coriander seeds. Add the crushed spices to the vegetables together with the bay leaf and a little salt. Pour in 1.5 litres/2½pints/6¼ cups water and bring to the boil. Simmer for about 20 minutes. Stir in the lime juice and wine. Take the pan off the heat, cover and leave in a cool place to infuse (steep) for 12 hours. Strain the stock through a fine sieve. It can be kept in the refrigerator for a day, or frozen.

LEMON DRESSING

I love this dressing, which is quick and easy to make. The lemon helps to intensify the flavours of salad leaves (greens).

MAKES 200ML/7FL OZ/SCANT 1 CUP

150ml/5fl oz/⅔ cup extra virgin olive oil
50ml/2fl oz/¼ cup lemon juice
salt and freshly ground pepper

Combine all the ingredients in a large bowl and whisk well.

BASIL OIL

MAKES 500ML/18FL OZ/2¼ CUPS

500g/1lb 2oz fresh basil
500ml/18fl oz/2¼ cups olive oil

Pick off the basil leaves and blanch in boiling water for 3 seconds. Refresh in iced water and squeeze dry. Blitz the basil and olive oil in a food processor for 5 minutes, then push through a chinois (bouillon strainer), making sure you extract every drop. Strain through a double thickness of coffee filter papers, store in Kilner (Mason) or other airtight jars. The oil will keep for up to 6 weeks.

PLUM CHUTNEY

MAKES ABOUT 1.5 LITRES/2½ PINTS/6¼ CUPS

1 kg/2¼lb plums, stoned (pitted)
250g/9oz/generous 1 cup soft brown sugar
500ml/18fl oz/2¼ cups malt vinegar
25g/1oz garlic, chopped
2 tbsp ground ginger
1 tbsp salt
2 tsp freshly ground black pepper
350g/12oz/2⅓ cups sultanas (golden raisins)

Place the plums, sugar and vinegar in a large pan and cook gently for about 30 minutes until the plums are soft.
Add the remaining ingredients and boil very gently, stirring occasionally, for about 1 hour, or until the mixture is thick. Pour into hot, clean jars and seal when cold.

Sauces

MAYONNAISE

MAKES ABOUT 1 LITRE/1¾ PINTS/4 CUPS

4 egg yolks
4 tsp Dijon mustard
50ml/2fl oz/¼ cup white wine vinegar
Worcestershire sauce
1 litre/1¾ pints/4 cups vegetable oil
salt and freshly ground pepper

In a food processor, combine the egg yolks, mustard and vinegar
with a dash of Worcestershire sauce and a little salt and pepper,
and mix well. With the motor running, gradually add the oil until it
has all been incorporated and the mayonnaise is thick and glossy.
Season to taste.

HOLLANDAISE

MAKES ABOUT 500ML/18FL OZ/2¼ CUPS

100ml/3½fl oz/scant ½ cup dry white wine
50ml/2fl oz/¼ cup white wine vinegar
100ml/3½fl oz/scant ½ cup water
12 white peppercorns, crushed
2 tsp chopped shallot
chervil, parsley and tarragon stalks
5 egg yolks
600g/1lb 5oz/ 2⅔ cups unsalted (sweet) butter
juice of ½ lemon
salt and freshly ground pepper

Put the white wine, vinegar, water, peppercorns, chopped shallot
and a few herb stalks in a pan over a medium heat. Reduce by
two-thirds, then leave to cool. Put the egg yolks in a heatproof bowl
and pass the cooled reduction on to the yolks.
Whisk in a bain-marie or over hot water with a balloon whisk until
the mixture is thick enough to coat the back of a spoon. Gently
melt the butter and skim the white sediment from the top. Leave to
cool to blood temperature. Whisk the cooled butter slowly into the
egg mixture. Season with lemon juice, salt and pepper.

BÉCHAMEL

MAKES ABOUT 600ML/1 PINT/ 2½ CUPS

40g/1½oz/3 tbsp unsalted (sweet) butter
50g/2oz/½ cup plain (all-purpose) flour
600ml/1 pint/2½ cups milk
1 small onion, peeled and studded with a bay leaf and 2 cloves
salt and freshly ground pepper

Melt the butter in a pan, add the flour and stir to make
a roux. Cook without colouring over a low heat for 5–6 minutes,
stirring constantly, then leave to cool.
Put the milk and onion in another pan, and bring just to boiling
point. Remove the onion and gradually pour the milk on
to the roux, stirring constantly to avoid lumps. Cook slowly over
a low heat for about 30 minutes. Pass the béchamel through
a fine sieve and season to taste.

MINT PESTO

MAKES ABOUT 300G/11OZ

15g/½oz/2 tbsp shelled pistachio nuts, skinned
50g/2oz/⅔ cup freshly grated Parmesan cheese
50g/2oz/2 cups mint leaves
25g/1oz/1 cup parsley sprigs
25g/1oz garlic, chopped
25g/1oz/¼ cup pine nuts
15g/½oz/2 tbsp walnut pieces
250ml/9fl oz/generous 1 cup olive oil
salt and freshly ground pepper

Put all the ingredients except the olive oil in a food processor. Add
half the oil and whizz until the ingredients are finely chopped. With
the motor running, gradually add the remaining oil through the
feeder tube until it is all incorporated. Season to taste.
Process again briefly.

SALSA VERDE (GREEN SAUCE)

MAKES 400ML/14FL OZ/1¾ CUPS

25g/1oz/1 cup flat parsley
25g/1oz/1 cup basil
50g/2oz/2 cups mint
1 garlic clove, peeled
1 tsp capers
1 anchovy fillet
2 tbsp red wine vinegar
200ml/7fl oz/scant 1 cup extra virgin olive oil
1 tsp Dijon mustard
salt and freshly ground pepper

Put the parsley, basil, mint, garlic, capers and anchovy in a food processor, and pulse until coarsely chopped. Add the vinegar, then, with the motor running, trickle in the oil in a steady stream. Whisk in the mustard and season with salt and pepper.

PEPPER SAUCE

50g/2oz/¼ cup finely chopped onions
3 tbsp oil
2 garlic cloves, crushed
2 tbsp black peppercorns, crushed
200ml/7fl oz/scant 1 cup white wine
300ml/10fl oz/1¼ cup Veal Jus (see page 181)
50g/2oz/¼ cup unsalted (sweet) butter
salt

In a pan, sweat the onions in the oil until soft and translucent, add the garlic and crushed peppercorns, and sweat for another minute. Add the white wine and reduce until syrupy. Add the veal jus and simmer for 10 minutes. Pass the sauce through a fine sieve. At the last moment, add the butter and whisk it into the sauce with a hand-held blender until completely amalgamated. Season with salt.

WHITE WINE SAUCE

MAKES ABOUT 500ML/18FL OZ/2¼ CUPS

2 tbsp chopped shallot
12 white peppercorns, crushed
100ml/3½fl oz/scant ½ cup dry white wine
200ml/7fl oz/scant 1 cup Fish Stock (see page 180)
100ml/3½fl oz/scant ½ cup Vegetable Stock (see page 182)
100ml/3½fl oz/scant ½ cup double (heavy) cream
cayenne pepper
salt

Put the shallot, peppercorns and white wine in a pan and reduce by two-thirds. Add the fish and vegetable stocks and again reduce by two-thirds. Add the cream and reduce by half. Season to taste with cayenne and salt.

CAULIFLOWER CREAM

25g/2oz/½ cup nibbed almonds
6 garlic cloves, peeled
300ml/10fl oz/1¼ cups milk
2 shallots, finely chopped
2 tbsp oil
2 cauliflowers, cut into small florets
2 tbsp sherry vinegar
300ml/10fl oz/1¼ cups Chicken Stock (see page 180)
200ml/7fl oz/scant 1 cup crème fraîche
juice of ½ lemon
salt and freshly ground pepper

Soak the almonds in cold water for 3 hours, changing the water twice. Blanch the garlic in the milk and an equal quantity of water; drain and repeat three times.
In a pan, sweat the shallots in the oil until soft and translucent. Add the cauliflower, almonds, blanched garlic and sherry vinegar, and reduce until almost all the vinegar has evaporated. Add the chicken stock and crème fraîche, and simmer until the cauliflower is soft. Whizz in a blender or food processor and pass through a fine sieve. Add a little lemon juice and season with salt and pepper.

Pastry and Dough

VANILLA SAUCE

MAKES ABOUT 600ML/1 PINT/2½ CUPS

500ml/18fl oz/2¼ cups milk
1 vanilla pod (bean), split lengthways
6 egg yolks
80g/3oz/scant ½ cup caster (superfine) sugar

Heat the milk and infuse (steep) the vanilla pod (bean) in it for about 10 minutes. Whisk the egg yolks and sugar together. Bring the milk to the boil, pour on to the egg yolk mixture and mix thoroughly. Pour the mixture into a clean pan and stir gently with a wooden spoon over a low heat until the sauce thickens and coats the back of a spoon. Leave to cool, then pass through a fine sieve.

CHOCOLATE SAUCE

MAKES ABOUT 600 ML/1 PINT/2½ CUPS

500ml/18 fl oz/2¼ cups water
350g/12 oz/1½ cups sugar
40g/1½ oz plain (semisweet) couverture
80g/3oz/¾ cup (unsweetened) cocoa powder
2 tbsp cornflour (cornstarch)

Put 300ml/10fl oz/1¼ cups of the water with 200g/7oz/scant 1 cup of the sugar and the couverture in a pan and simmer until the chocolate has melted. Mix the (unsweetened) cocoa powder with the remaining water and sugar and stir into the simmering chocolate mixture.

RASPBERRY SAUCE

SERVES 4

300g/11oz/scant 2 cups raspberries, hulled
2 tsp lemon juice
40g/1½oz/⅓ cup icing (confectioners') sugar

Purée the raspberries in a blender or food processor, then add the lemon juice and sugar. Pass the sauce through a fine sieve or muslin (cheesecloth) into a bowl, and chill until needed.

STOCK SYRUP

MAKES ABOUT 1 LITRE/1¾ PINTS/4 CUPS

400g/14oz/2 cups caster (superfine) sugar
900ml/1½ pints/3¾ cups water
100ml/3½fl oz/scant ½ cup white wine
juice of ½ lemon
2 vanilla pods (beans), split lengthways

Heat the sugar, water and wine with the lemon juice, bring to the boil and strain through a fine sieve or muslin (cheesecloth. Scrape in the inside of the vanilla pods (beans) and stir well.
Put the vanilla pods in a jar of sugar to infuse (steep) and create vanilla-scented sugar to use in desserts.

PASTRY CREAM

MAKES ABOUT 1 LITRE/1¾ PINTS/4 CUPS

1 litre/1¾ pints/4 cups milk
1 vanilla pod (bean), split lengthways
8 egg yolks
200g/7oz/1 cup sugar
40g/1½oz/⅓ cup flour
40g/1½oz/scant ¼ cup cornflour (cornstarch)

Bring the milk to the boil with the vanilla pod (bean). Whisk together the egg yolks, sugar, flour and cornflour (cornstarch). Pour the boiling milk on to this mixture and whisk well. Return the mixture to the pan, bring back to the boil and continue whisking for about 1 minute. Chill the pastry cream as quickly as possible.

SWEET SHORTCRUST PASTRY

225g/8oz/1 cup unsalted butter, softened
100g/4oz/½ cup caster (superfine) sugar
1 egg, beaten
350g/8oz/3 cups plain (all-purpose) flour, plus extra for dusting
pinch of salt

Cream the butter and sugar together until very pale. Slowly beat in the egg. Gradually add the flour and salt and mix to a smooth paste. Cover and leave to rest in the refrigerator before using.

PUFF PASTRY

MAKES ABOUT 1.3KG/2LB 14OZ

675g/1½lb/6 cups plain (all-purpose) flour
675g/1½lb/3 cups unsalted (sweet) butter
1½ tsp salt
275 ml/9 fl oz/generous 1 cup iced water
juice of ½ lemon

Put 175g/6oz/1½ cups of the flour on a cool surface and make a well. Put in 500g/1lb 2oz/2¼ cups of the butter and work it into the flour until thoroughly mixed. Form into a 12.5cm/5in square block, 4cm/1½in thick, and chill.

Rub the remaining butter into the remaining flour with the salt until the mixture resembles fine breadcrumbs. Add the iced water and lemon juice, and mix to form a dough. Knead until smooth and elastic. Shape the dough into a small ball, then make 2 incisions in the shape of a cross to one-third of the depth of the dough. Open out the points and roll out each one into a 12.5cm/5in square, about 5mm/¼ in thick. Place the butter and flour block in the centre of this dough, and fold over the flaps, working anticlockwise (counterclockwise), making sure that the edges are well sealed.

Roll the dough into 30 x 60cm/12 x 24in rectangle. Fold in the short sides to meet in the middle, then fold the dough in half to form 4 equal layers; this process is called a "double turn". Cover with a damp cloth and leave to rest in the refrigerator for at least 30 minutes.

Repeat the process 4 times. Finally, cover the dough and leave it to rest in the refrigerator for several hours, preferably overnight.

FLEURONS

MAKES 4

Roll out 40g/1½oz puff pastry to a 3mm/⅛in thickness, rolling it in different directions to prevent distortion during cooking. Use a 6cm/2½in pastry (cookie) cutter to stamp out 4 crescent shapes, or make any shapes you like. Place on a greased baking tray (cookie sheet), brush the tops with egg yolk and, if you like, sprinkle with poppy or sesame seeds. Chill for 20 minutes. Heat the oven to 200°C/400°F/Gas Mark 6 and bake the fleurons for about 15 minutes until golden brown.

RAVIOLI DOUGH

The only difference between ravioli dough and basic pasta dough is the increased quantity of egg yolks, which gives it more softness and flexibility. If you want to make tagliatelle, use only 3 egg yolks but add an extra whole egg.

MAKES ABOUT 450G/1LB

250g/9oz/2¼ cups Italian tipo 00 flour,
  plus extra for dusting
¼ tsp salt
2 whole eggs
5 egg yolks
1 tbsp olive oil

Sift the flour. Combine all the ingredients in a food processor and process to obtain a well-mixed dough. Turn the dough on to a well-floured surface and knead for 5–10 minutes, or until the dough is very smooth and elastic.

Shape the dough into a ball, cover and leave to rest in a cool place for 1 hour.

Cut the dough into pieces about the size of a lemon. Work with 1 piece at a time, keeping the remaining dough covered.

Set a pasta maker on its widest setting. Feed through a piece of dough several times, folding the sheet of dough each time, until it is smooth and elastic. To roll out the dough, set the rollers to the next narrowest setting and feed the dough through. Set the machine down another notch, and feed the dough through again, this time without folding it. Continue until you reach the setting specified in the recipe.

If the pasta dough is to be used for lasagne or filled shapes, such as tortellini or ravioli, cut it as soon as it is rolled out. If it is to be used for tagliatelle or other noodles, leave it to dry for about 20 minutes before cutting.

Vegetable Dishes and Salads

FRANGIPANE

120g/4oz/½ cup unsalted (sweet) butter, softened
120g/4 oz/1 cup icing (confectioners') sugar
5 large (extra large eggs), beaten
25g/1oz/¼ cup plain (all-purpose) flour
120g/4oz/1 cup ground almonds
4 tsp dark rum

Cream the softened butter with the icing (confectioners') sugar, then gradually beat in the eggs. Sift the flour and ground almonds, and stir them into the butter mixture until smooth, then stir in the rum.

CHOUX PASTE

MAKES ABOUT 275G/10OZ

125ml/4fl oz/½ cup milk
50g/2oz/½ cup unsalted (sweet) butter
65g/2½oz/⅔ cup plain (all-purpose) flour, sifted
2 eggs
salt

Boil the milk with the butter until the butter has melted. Reduce the heat, add the flour and salt and stir well until the mixture forms a smooth paste. Cook for 2–3 minutes, stirring constantly. Transfer the paste to a bowl and beat in the eggs, 1 at a time. Use while still slightly warm.

SAVOY WILD MUSHROOM MIXTURE

SERVES 4

10g/¼oz black trumpet mushrooms
25g/1oz chanterelle mushrooms
40g/1½oz girolle mushrooms
25g/1oz pieds de mouton (hedgehog mushrooms)
1½ tbsp finely chopped shallot
2 tbsp olive oil
1 garlic clove garlic, crushed
fresh herbs, to suit the recipe
salt and freshly ground pepper

Trim the mushrooms and cut them into 1cm/½in pieces if they are very large. Briefly wash, then blanch in boiling water for 20 seconds. Refresh in iced water and drain.
In a frying pan (skillet), sweat the chopped shallot in the oil until soft and translucent, add the garlic and sweat for another minute. Add the blanched mushrooms, season and add the appropriate herb. Cook for about 2 minutes to reheat the mushrooms.

MEDITERRANEAN VEGETABLES

SERVES 4

2 red (bell) peppers
100ml/3½fl oz/scant ½ cup olive oil
1 onion, finely chopped
2 garlic cloves, chopped into a fine paste
100g/3½oz mushrooms, quartered
2 courgettes (zucchini), cut into 1cm/½in cubes
1 small rosemary sprig
2 tsp sugar
2 tsp white wine vinegar
4 ripe but firm plum tomatoes, peeled, de-seeded
  and cut into1cm/½in cubes
salt and freshly ground pepper

Heat the oven to 220°C/425°F/Gas Mark 7. Rub the (bell) peppers with a little olive oil and put them in a small casserole or roasting tin (pan). Cover with a lid or foil and bake for 20 minutes. Remove the casserole or tin from the oven and set aside, covered, for 10 minutes. Lower the oven temperature to 180°C/350°F/Gas Mark 4.
When the peppers are cool enough to handle, peel them. Discard the stalks, ribs and seeds and cut the flesh into 1cm/½in squares.

Heat the remaining olive oil in a flameproof casserole and cook the onion over a low heat until soft and translucent, stirring frequently. Add the garlic and cook for 1 minute longer.

Add the mushrooms and courgettes (zucchini) to the casserole and cook for 2 minutes, stirring occasionally. Add the red peppers to the casserole and stir well. Add the rosemary, sugar and vinegar, and season with salt and pepper. Cover the casserole and transfer to the oven. Cook for 25 minutes, stirring frequently.

Stir the tomatoes into the ragoût. Taste and adjust the seasoning and discard the rosemary sprig before serving.

RADISH SALAD

SERVES 4

25g/1oz/⅓ cup julienne of spring onions (scallions)
25g/1oz/scant ¼ cup julienne of carrots
25g/1oz/scant ¼ cup julienne of radish
25g/1oz/1 cup flat leaf parsley or coriander (cilantro) leaves
50ml/2fl oz/¼ cup Lemon Dressing (see page 182)

Mix everything together.

OLIVE OIL POTATO PURÉE

SERVES 4

675g/1½lb potatoes
150ml/5fl oz/⅔ cup extra virgin olive oil
18 garlic cloves, peeled
4 tbsp milk
5 tbsp double (heavy) cream
salt and freshly ground pepper

Peel the potatoes and cut them into large cubes. Place in a pan, just cover with cold water, and add one-third of the olive oil, all the garlic cloves and salt to taste. Bring to the boil and simmer for 15–20 minutes until the potatoes are tender but not mushy. Drain. Put the garlic cloves on a board and crush with the flat of a knife. Heat 1 tbsp of the remaining olive oil in a frying pan (skillet) over a medium heat and cook the garlic for 1 minute. Do not allow it to colour. Return the garlic to the potatoes and press through a fine sieve into a bowl, or use a potato ricer or masher.

Heat the milk, cream and remaining oil in a pan. Slowly add the potatoes, mixing well with a wooden spoon. Season and serve.

Ice Creams

VANILLA ICE CREAM

MAKES ABOUT 400ML/14FL OZ/1¾ CUPS

25g/1oz/scant ¼ cup milk powder (dry milk)
500ml/18fl oz/2¼ cups milk
300ml/10fl oz/1¼ cups double (heavy) cream
1 vanilla pod (bean), split
5 egg yolks
100g/3½oz/½ cup caster (superfine) sugar

Mix the milk powder (dry milk) to a thick paste with a little of the milk, then stir in the remaining milk. Add this mixture to the cream and bring to the boil with the split vanilla pod (bean). Take off the heat and leave to infuse (steep) for 15 minutes.

Remove the vanilla pod from the milk. Whisk the egg yolks and sugar together, pour on the flavoured milk, and mix well. Pour the mixture into a clean pan and cook over a very gentle heat, stirring constantly with a wooden spoon until the mixture becomes thick and coats the back of the spoon. It is important not to boil the mixture at this stage, or it will separate. Cool and pass through a fine sieve.

Churn in an ice cream maker to a light consistency. Place the ice cream in the freezer for 2 hours until firm and ready to scoop

BASIL ICE CREAM

MAKES ABOUT 250G/9OZ/2 CUPS

300ml/10fl oz/1¼ cups milk
25g/1oz/1 cup basil, washed and coarsely chopped
160ml/5½fl oz/generous ⅔ cup whipping cream
50g/2oz/¼ cup sugar
5 egg yolks

Boil the milk and add half the basil. Boil the cream with the sugar and add it to the milk

Whisk the egg yolks and the remaining sugar until pale and creamy. Stir in the boiling milk and cream, pour the mixture into a clean pan, and bring to the boil, stirring constantly with a wooden spoon. Cook until the mixture is slightly thickened and coats the back of the spoon.

Leave to cool completely, then churn in an ice cream maker. Alternatively, pour the mixture into a large freezer proof bowl, cover and freeze until almost set. Transfer to a food processor and whizz to break down the ice crystals. Return the mixture to the bowl, add the remaining basil, cover and freeze again for 3 hours until almost set. Repeat the process once more to obtain a very smooth ice cream.

To serve: If the ice cream has been kept in the freezer for a while and has gone hard, transfer it to the refrigerator for 20–30 minutes before serving to soften it slightly.

BURNT ORANGE ICE CREAM

MAKES ABOUT 900ML/1½ PINTS/3¾ CUPS

1 vanilla pod (bean), split
200ml/7fl oz/scant 1 cup milk
200ml/7fl oz/scant 1 cup whipping cream
6 egg yolks
200g/7oz/scant 1 cup sugar
80g/3oz/scant ½ cup caster (superfine) sugar
200ml/7fl oz/scant 1 cup water
3 tbsp Grand Marnier
300ml/10fl oz/1¼ cups orange juice, reduced to a syrup

Scrape the inside of the vanilla pod (bean) into the milk and bring to the boil. Take the pan off the heat and leave to infuse (steep) for 15 minutes. In another pan, boil the cream, then add it to the milk.
To make the custard: In a bowl, cream the egg yolks and sugar until pale. Pour on the hot milk mixture, stirring constantly. Return the custard to the pan and stir over a low heat until it coats the back of a spoon. Pass through a fine sieve and cool quickly.
Put the caster (superfine) sugar in a dry pan and cook to a very dark, almost burnt caramel. Take the pan off the heat and stir in the water, Grand Marnier and reduced orange juice.
Simmer until syrupy, then cool.
Whisk the orange syrup into the custard and churn in an ice cream maker.

CINNAMON ICE CREAM

MAKES ABOUT 500ML/18FL OZ/2¼ CUPS

400ml/14fl oz/1¾ cups milk
1 vanilla pod (bean)
7 egg yolks
80g/3 oz scant ½ cup caster (superfine) sugar

FOR THE CINNAMON CREAM

1 litre/1¾ pints/4 cups double (heavy) cream
2½ very fresh cinnamon sticks

Pour the milk in to a heavy pan. Split the vanilla pod (bean) open and add to the milk. Heat until bubbles form around the edge. Remove from the heat and leave in a warm place to infuse (steep) for 10 minutes.
Meanwhile, whisk the egg yolks with the sugar in a bowl. Set the bowl over a pan of hot water and whisk until the sugar has dissolved and the mixture is pale, thick and increased in volume. Incorporate half the warm milk, whisking well.
Heat the milk remaining in the pan to just below simmering point. Gradually add the milk and egg yolk mixture in a steady stream, stirring constantly with a wooden spoon. Cook over a low heat, stirring, until the custard thickens enough to coat the back of the spoon thinly. Strain it through a fine sieve into a bowl, and set the bowl in a container of iced water to prevent further cooking. Leave the custard to cool.
To make the cinnamon cream: Combine the cream with the fresh cinnamon sticks in a pan. Bring to the boil, and boil until reduced by half. Strain the cream and leave it to cool.
Mix together the cooled vanilla custard and cinnamon cream in a large freezerproof bowl. Cover and freeze for 2 hours or until the mixture begins to firm up. Transfer the half-frozen ice cream to a blender or food processor, and whizz until it is smooth and creamy, and the ice crystals have broken down. Pour it back into the bowl, cover and return to the freezer. Freeze until the ice cream firms up again, then whizz in the blender or food processor as before. Cover and freeze again, whizz once more, then freeze until firm. The ice cream is now ready for serving.
If the ice cream is kept in the freezer and has frozen very hard, transfer it to the refrigerator 20–30 minutes before serving to soften it slightly.

Index

Acknowledgements

Nothing good is ever achieved without enthusiasm. For showing that essential quality in abundance and for their dedication and hard work I thank all the colleagues and friends who helped me with this book.

My special thanks to the Director and General Manager of The Savoy, Mr Michael Shepherd for his help and generosity. My thanks and gratitude to the chefs in The Savoy restaurant kitchen, especially Holgar Jackisch, Ian Thomason, Martin Nisbet, Rodger Manning, Robert Hope and all the others who showed so much patience, understanding and goodwill.

My PA, Rebecca Todd, Kate Whiteman, Lizzy Gray and Barbara Levy were all of immeasurable help to me.

My thanks to them, and last, but very far from least, to my wife Sue, for all her tremendous encouragement.

First published in Great Britain in 2003 by PAVILION BOOKS LIMITED
The Chrysalis Building, Bramley Road, W10 6SP
www.chrysalisbooks.co.uk

An imprint of Chrysalis Books Group plc

Text © Anton Edelmann and Kate Whiteman, 2003
Photographs © Jean Cazal, 2003, except where stated below
Design and layout © Pavilion Books Ltd., 2003

The moral right of the authors has been asserted.

Design: Andrew Barron at thextension
Senior Commissoning Editor: Stuart Cooper
Editor: Lizzy Gray

The Publishers would like to thank the following picture libraries for permission to reproduce images: p98 © Hulton-Deutsch Collection/Corbis; pp12-13, 82, 166 © Hulton|Archive.

A CIP catalogue record for this book is available from the British Library

ISBN 1 86205 387 1

Colour origination by Classicscan Pte Ltd (Singapore)
Printed by Imago Publishing (Singapore)

1 2 3 4 5 6 7 8 9 10

This book can be ordered direct from the publisher. Please contact the Marketing Department. But try your bookshop first.